A Storm Is Coming

©Forgotten Heroes 14-19 Limited

The Unknown Fallen

History tends to shy away from discussing how individuals are involved in the course of time. The starting point is more often listing the events and battles that are relevant instead of addressing how people personally experienced the events. This is the case for the First World War.

The Forgotten Heroes 14-19 Foundation hopes to foster dialogues which are truly transnational, multicultural and interfaith, between peoples of different nations, religions, languages and identities. The aim is to find a common humanity based on universal values.

As various forms of conflict, war and terrorism, have become prominent topics in recent years it is important that we pay attention to how people have viewed and dealt with events like the First World War. Understanding the human aspect of conflict is important as it not only gives one an understanding of the real consequences of certain actions, it helps us understand better why things are the way they are.

The Forgotten Heroes 14-19 Foundation has discovered that, based on original documents, at least 2,5 million Muslim soldiers and laborers from all over the world, fought with the Allied forces with dignity and honor, many of whom were more decorated than their European counterparts.

Muslim, Christian, Hindu, Sikh, Jewish, of all faiths and none, soldiers fought united, side-by-side; sharing their experiences, and accommodating each other's cultures, music, gastronomy and religious practices, despite the difficult conditions wherever they served.

It is essential to uncover and understand what happened in the past and to reinforce the stories of solidarity as well as suffering, thus similar scenes are not repeated.

We sincerely hope that this introductory coffee table book will generate global interest within communities of all faiths and none and convince you to look deeper into the personal stories of these men.

Luc Ferier
Chairman & Founder
Forgotten Heroes 14-19 Foundation
www.muslimsinww1.com
www.unknowfallen.com

> Grown-ups never understand
> anything for themselves,
> and it is tiresome for children
> to be always and forever
> explaining things to them.
> — Antoine de Saint-Exupéry

Men Of The Earth

I wandered through graveyards of thousands who died
Each tombstone a great weight on my chest
Mourning how death had come to reside
On young men at Notre Damme de Lorette

The silent breeze swept eerily through trees with ease
Over lush greens farmlands, pockmarked by war
The cannon fodder of beloved sons laid to rest in peace
Blooded bodies now sacred seedling for earth

Had they longed for their homes in far away lands
Thought of monsoon rains and desert hot plains
Craved the tender touch of mothers and wives?
In this climate so foreign and hostile

With what ease had they befriended fellow fighting men
Embracing difference to create brotherhoods,
How did their faith bring them closer to rely on each other
While around them trenches were bombed till they shook?

Colonized, conscripted or dutifully bound
They faced bravely the baptisms of artillery fire
As trench builders, soldiers, doctors and gunners,
Destroying the labyrinths of enemy wires

From all over the world, men were drafted in droves
No crosses, crescents or stars to divide them
These comrades requested to be buried in tow
To the men who had fought right beside them

Relentless rain of grenades, gunfire, shrapnel and gas
Obeying orders to advance, to defend or attack
Witnessing deaths of their comrades, buried in mass graves
What terrors must these young men have faced?

In photos, sepia sons stand solemnly side by side
A ghostly brotherhood forever suspended in time
Their bodies rising like mist from the earth
From the frontlines to be seen, named, their voices heard

Each one commemorated, to truly honour their lives
The reveal of true history so they're remembered in time
How men joined forces, regardless of colour or creed
A myriad of nationalities stood together in good stead

Amongst the lush fields of forget-me-nots and red poppies
I pray for the day I only see poppies of white
Standing amongst the east-facing headstones and crosses
Hoping wars are replaced with humanity and light

Hafsah Aneela Bashir

> *If you don't know history, then you don't know anything. You are a leaf that doesn't know it is part of a tree.*

Contents

1-2	*25-26*	*49-50*	*73-74*
Introduction	Islam	"Tears are words the	"Just because you
"We may have different religions..."		heart can't say."	don't understand..."
3-4	*27-28*	*51-52*	*75-76*
"Grown-ups never understand	"None of us knows what might	"God will not look you over	"Nothing in this world is harder than
anything for themselves..."	happen even the next minute..."	for medals or degrees..."	speaking the truth..."
5-6	*29-30*	*53-54*	*77-78*
Contents	"Which charity is best?"	"I cannot teach	"When you are laboring
"If you don't know history..."		anybody anything..."	for others..."
7-8	*31-32*	*55-56*	*79-80*
"Facts do not cease to exist	"Compassion is the	"One cannot and must not try to	"From trenches deep
because they are ignored."	basis of morality."	erase the Allied Muslim..."	towards the sky..."
9-10	*33-34*	*57-58*	*81-82*
"The living owe it to those who	"May the magic of Eid	"These documents will foster a new	"The death of an elderly man
no longer can speak to tell..."	bring lots of happiness..."	found pride & confidence..."	is like a burning library."
11-12	*35-36*	*59-60*	*83-84*
Algeria	"Don't walk in front of me,	"Where there is loyalty,	"Wisdom is like a baobab tree;
	I may not follow..."	weapons are of no use."	no one individual can embrace it."
13-14	*37-38*	*61-62*	*85-86*
Senegal	"There are as many minds	"I have accepted fear	"I learned that courage
	as there are heads..."	as part of my life..."	was not the absence of fear..."
15-16	*39-40*	*63-64*	*87-88*
Baluchistan	"If I can see pain in your eyes..."	"I could hear my heart beating. I could	"Commemorating World War 1
	"I don't want to be rich..."	hear everyone's heart beating..."	is not about military victory..."
17-18	*41-42*	*65-66*	*89-90*
Tunisia	"In Diversity there is beauty	"A sense of the universe,	"Remember that these men
	and there is strength."	a sense of the all..."	are not just statistics..."
19-20	*43-44*	*67-68*	*91-102*
Somalia	"If we cannot end now	"Then the heat of Arabia came	Brothers in Arms
	our differences..."	out like a drawn sword..."	
21-22	*45-46*	*69-70*	*103-104*
Morocco	"The greatness of humanity	"If you tell the truth you don't have to	"If not us, then who?
	is not in being human..."	remember anything."	If not now, then when?"
23-24	*47-48*	*71-72*	*105-106*
India	"Don't envy my smile because	"The true soldier fights	"The most effective way
	it took me a lot of tears to get it..."	not because he hates..."	to destroy people is to deny..."

Statistics

Several articles have laid bare the public's lack of knowledge of the reach and impact of the 1914-18 conflict, and this after years of commemoration events.

A study in 2014 found that in the UK, not even half the 1,081 people questioned were aware that North America and the Middle East played a part in the First World War (38% and 34% respectively), while less than a quarter realised that Africa and Asia were involved (21% and 22%).

Less than a third of UK respondents associated the war with the fall of the Ottoman Empire (32%), the creation of the United Nations (27%), and only 11% were aware of its connection with the ongoing conflict between Israel and the Palestinians.

Questions relating to the divide of Africa after the First World War, which potentially led to the Rwanda genocide of the 1990s, were not even asked.

John Worne, director of strategy at the British Council, said: *"Our research shows that the things we in the United Kingdom know and remember the most from the First World War are the harrowing images and iconic stories from the Western Front, where most of the British soldiers died. But the British people shouldn't forget that the war touched many other parts of the world. Far more countries fought and were affected than we generally think."*

The enormous gap in the general knowledge of the international community about how global the First World War was, the fighting on the Russian front, the Balkans, Middle East, Mesopotamia, South and West Africa, and the involvement of all cultures and religions, needs to be addressed urgently.

In the centenary year of the Balfour Declaration,* we cannot deny the fact that there are critical conflicts in several regions that still have to be resolved, and we cannot deny our part in them.

Military Casualties: The Robert Schuman European Centre(CERS)**
http://www.centre-robert-schuman.org

Allied powers	Staff mobilized	Killed in action	Wounded in action	Total casualties	Casualties as % of total mobilized
Australia	412,953	61,928	152,171	214,099	52 %
Belgium	267,000	38,172	44,686	82,858	31 %
Canada	628,964	64,944	149,732	214,676	34 %
France	8,410,000	1,397,800	4,266,000	5,663,800	67 %
Greece	230,000	26,000	21,000	47,000	20 %
India	1,440,437	74,187	69,214	143,401	10 %
Italy	5,615,000	651,010	953,886	1,604,896	29 %
Japan	800,000	415	907	1,322	< 1 %
Montenegro	50,000	3,000	10,000	13,000	26 %
Nepal	200,000	30,000	?	?	?
New Zealand	128,525	18,050	41,317	59,367	46 %
Portugal	100,000	7,222	13,751	20,973	21 %
Romania	750,000	250,000	120,000	370,000	49 %
Russia	12,000,000	1,811,000	4,950,000	6,761,000	56 %
Serbia	707,343	275,000	133,148	408,148	58 %
South Africa	136,070	9,463	12,029	21,492	16 %
United Kingdom	6,211,922	886,342	1,665,749	2,552,091	41 %
United States of America	4,355,000	116,708	205,690	322,398	7 %
Total	42,243,214	5,691,241	12,809,280	18,500,521	44 %

*https://www.britannica.com/event/Balfour-Declaration
**Numbers are lower than in 2017 due to previously unaccounted groups as laborers. Locally recruited soldiers and laborers who participated in the war are unaccounted for.

Legend:
- UNITED KINGDOM
- FRANCE
- GERMANY
- ITALY
- SPAIN
- PORTUGAL
- BELGIUM
- INDEPENDENT

Territories labelled on map:
Spanish Morocco, Morocco, Tunisia, Algeria, Libya, Rio de Oro, Egypt, French West Africa, Eritrea, Gambia, Port Guinea, Anglo-Egyptian Sudan, French Somalia, Sierra Leone, Gold Coast, Nigeria, Ethiopia, British Somalia, Liberia, Togoland, Cameroon, Italian Somaliland, Spanish Guinea, Uganda, French Equatorial Africa, Kenya, Belgian Congo, German East Africa, Angola, Nyasaland, Northern Rodesia, Mozambique, Madagascar, German Southwest Africa, Southern Rodesia, Bechuanaland, Swaziland, Basutoland, South Africa

CARTE GÉNÉRALE DE L'AFRIQUE

> *Facts do not cease to exist because they are ignored.*
> — Aldous Huxley

Allied Entente powers

Allied colonies, dominions or occupied territory

Central powers

Central powers' colonies or occupied territory

Neutral

Thousands of books have been written on the war in Europe and research done on the battles, however little is known about the exhausting, deadly journeys soldiers and laborers from across the world made to the front lines and...back home.

Contingents were moved from Asia across Canada towards the United Kingdom before arriving in Europe. Others were transported via South Africa or the Suez canal.

Soldiers from the Caribbean froze to death on board transport ships, Chinese and South African laborers were torpedoed in the Mediterranean sea and off the Isle of Wright respectively.

Diaspora journeys were amazing frightening adventures.

— 9 —

©Forgotten Heroes 14-19 Limited

The living owe it to those who no longer can speak to tell their story for them.

April 1917

Algeria

Mohamed Osman (Spahi) Muslim
Algerian Trooper (from Oran)

The word Spahi conjures up an extravagant fantasy, rifle shots, white smoke under a blue sky, dazzling sun, frenzied galloping, flame colored burnous flying. The Algerian troopers played their part in the conflict and the war took everything from them: their red tunic was replaced by dull khaki, their joyous fusillade by a bitter and risky struggle behind the chain of fortifications; their life of sunshine and ardor by the dismal depressing existence of the trenches. They were sent to the flattest sector, in Flanders, a landscape constantly veiled in mist or drowning in rain.

When they came back from the front lines, they exercised their horses on the sandy dunes on the edge of the grey sea, and the bitter wind made their cloaks billow. Among all the trials and dangers they kept their calm, their fatalism, and the enduring dignity of their profile. And now the campaign is over, those who have been spared tell interminable stories under the palm trees of their villages, of their memories of the war and the strange life they led, the terrible paths followed by those of their sons whom Allah received into the Paradise of the Brave.*

Qui dit spahi, dit fantasia, coups de fusil, fumée blanche sous le ciel bleu, soleil éclatant, galop frénétique, envol de burnous couleur de feu. Les spahis sont venus à leur place de combat et la guerre leur a tout pris. De leur tunique rouge, elle a fait une triste vareuse kaki; de leur joyeuse fusillade, une lutte âpre et sournoise derrière la meurtrière d'un créneau; de leur vie de soleil, d'ardeur, de flamme, la morne, la déprimante existence des tranchées. On les a envoyés dans le secteur le plus plat, celui des Flandres, dans un paysage sans cesse voilé de brume ou noyé de pluie.

Quand ils descendaient des premières lignes, ils promenaient leurs chevaux sur les dunes blondes, au bord de la mer grise et l'âpre vent du large faisait voler leurs burnous. Parmi toutes les épreuves, tous les dangers, ils ont gardé leur calme, leur fatalisme et l'éternelle majesté de leur silhouette. Et maintenant, la campagne finie, ceux qu'elle a épargnés, racontent interminablement, sous les palmiers des douars, leurs souvenirs de la guerre et l'étrange vie qu'ils ont menée, et les terribles chemins qu'ont dû suivre ceux de ses fils qu'Allah a reçu dans le Paradis des Braves.

*The English translation is based on the original notes from the artist, written between 1915 and 1919 and even if some testimonies may sound awkward for people today, the painter was in full admiration of the men he painted and meant no offence in any way.

Eugène Burnand

Senegalese Rifleman
Famory (from Flala, canton of Bougoumé, Sudan)

A long profile with clear delineated features, a fine nose, high forehead, proud face, noble. He was born into a warrior aristocracy, for whom warfare is the raison d'être for living, and who had no other goal in life but to see his enemy laid low on the ground. He had been shown an enemy more powerful than all those he had previously fought, or whom he could even imagine. It was explained to him that an enemy of France was his enemy too, and that all he had to do was attack with a bayonet rather than the spear he was used to. He went off and fought, obeying blindly the orders given by his officers, and thus he proved worthy of his nation, his traditions, his ancestors, loyal just like him, and like him devoted and warlike.*

Long profil aux traits nettement détachés, le nez fin, le front haut, visage fier, marqué d'une sorte de majesté. Il est né d'une aristocratie guerrière, pour qui le combat est la raison d'être dela vie et qui n'a d'autre but en ce monde que de voir son ennemi à terre. On lui a montré un adversaire nouveau plus puissant, plus redoutable que tous ceux qu'il avait eu à combattre, que tous ceux qu'il pouvait même imaginer. On lui a expliqué que l'ennemi de la France était le sien propre et qu'il ne s'agissait plus de l'attaquer à coups de javelots, mais à la pointe de la baïonnette. Il est parti, il s'est battu, sans comprendre autre chose que l'ordre donné par ses officiers et ainsi il a bien mérité de sa race, de ses traditions, de ses ancêtres, loyaux comme lui et comme lui fanatiques et guerriers.

*The English translation is based on the original notes from the artist, written between 1915 and 1919 and even if some testimonies may sound awkward for people today, the painter was in full admiration of the men he painted and meant no offence in any way.

Eugène Burnand

Auxiliary from Baluchistan
Chan Mohamed

He has crowned his fierce-looking head with a green turban, so that everyone can see he is a believer and that he has travelled across the desert to pay homage to the tomb of the Prophet. So he is a believer, but not a zealot, less of a theologian than a soldier, and a soldier in a holy war. He comes from the rugged plateaus of Baluchistan, where the great wind of the Himalaya blows. Wild country with endless horizons, broken by walls of rock, a poor country, barren, without greenery or woods, covered with short grass grazed by flocks of sheep, land of shepherds, of nomads endlessly driving their animals before them, anxious about the next raid, a country of magnificent soldiers, merciless, brought up in the school of warfare since childhood. However they submitted their independence to harsh British discipline; these mountain men, used to wide open spaces and the sky, knew how to live the life required in this war of stagnation, right to the end, because a promise of fidelity had to be kept, and one could never break an oath made out loud and from the heart in the Holy City, in front of the tomb of the Prophet.*

Il a coiffé sa tête farouche du turban vert et ainsi chacun peut voir qu'il est un croyant et qu'à travers le désert il a été apporter l'hommage de sa foi au tombeau du Prophète. Donc croyant, mais point dévôt, moins théologien que soldat et soldat de guerre sainte. Il vient de ces rudes platueux du Beloutchistan où souffle le grand vent de l'Hymalaya. Pays sauvage, d'horizon illimité, coupés de pans de roche, pays pauvre, sans grâce, sans verdure, sans bois, fleuri d'une herbe courte que paissent les troupeaux, pays de bergers, de nomades poussant sans cesse devant eux leurs bêtes, inquiets de la razzia prochaine et pays de soldats magnifiques, impitoyables, élevés depuis l'enfance à l'école de la guerre. Ils ont cependant plié leur indépendance à la sévère discipline britannique: ces montagnards habitués à l'espace, au ciel, ont su mener danscette guerre de stagnation, la vie qu'il fallait, jusqu'au bout, parce qu'une promesse de fidélité doit être tenue et qu'on ne saurait parjurer un sermentfait de bouche et de coeur dans la Ville Sainte, devant le tombeau du Prophète.

– 15 –

©Forgotten Heroes 14-19 Limited

Baluchistan

*The English translation is based on the original notes from the artist, written between 1915 and 1919 and even if some testimonies may sound awkward for people today, the painter was in full admiration of the men he painted and meant no offence in any way.

Tunisia

Eugène Burnand

Tunisian Auxiliary
Mohamed Ben Nadroc (from Jadary)

Allah alone is great, chants the shrill voice of the muezzin, floating over the roofs of the white buildings of Tunis. Allah is great, when he orders faithful adherence to oaths. From the old city they came in crowds, the sons of Mohammed, whom our enemies hoped would revolt or prove treacherous. But these were not slaves, anxious to shake off their yoke, nor auxiliaries on the lookout for the first sign of weakness. They were brave soldiers whose hearts were without subterfuge. Tunisia, where silver olive trees shaded fruitful vines, where mines gave up their treasures; Tunisia the bountiful and rich gave more than the heavenly produce of her soil: she gave her children. The strident nouba, the military music, kept their feet in rhythm along all the routes of the front, in all the villages of France, bruised and desolate. Their silhouettes in bronze helmets were massed at all the points of departure. They shared all the sufferings; they earned the right to unalloyed honor.*

Allah seul est grand: chante la voix pointue de muezzin, sur les toits de Tunis la blanche. Allah est grand qui ordonne la fidélité aux serments. Dela vieille ville ils sont venus en foule, les fils de Mohammed, ceux que nos ennemis espéraient révoltés ou perfides. Ce n'étaient pas des esclaves impatients de secouer le joug, ni des auxiliaires à l'affût de la première défaillance. C'étaient de braves soldats à l'âme sans détour. La Tunisie où les oliviers d'argent ombragent des vignes généreuses, où les mines regorgent de trésors, la Tunisie grasse et riche a donné mieux que les divins produits de son sol: elle a donné ses enfants. La nouba stridente a rythmé leurs pas sur toutes les routes du front, dans tous les villages de france, meurtris et désolés. Leurs silhouettes casquées de bronze se sont massées dans toutes les souffrances: ils ont droit à la gloire sans mélange.

The English translation is based on the original notes from the artist, written between 1915 and 1919 and even if some testimonies may sound awkward for people today, the painter was in full admiration of the men he painted and meant no offence in any way.

Ahmed Abokob (Muslim)
Somali (from Djibouti)

The little serpentine head with shiny skin seems, under the blue steel helmet, animated by a strange life. The man does not have the powerful features of so many other dark-skinned men, nor their broad stature, nor their appearance of brutal and massive strength: he is lithe, light and no doubt skillful in all the tricks of war. He has always lived under the oppressive sun of Djibouti, on the edge of the sea, which seems to roll with fire. He has lived like a lizard on a rock, seemingly motionless, but quick to defend himself, agile when danger comes. At the gates of the desert, in one of those bastions with which France stakes out its distant routes, he has always seen our colors floating against the implacable blue sky; he followed them under the greyness of our climate, through the snow and the rain. His bronzed face has contracted under the great blast of shellfire, but his warrior blood has not shivered, nor has his faithfulness to our service wavered.*

Cette petite tête serpentine à la peau luisante semble, sous l'acier bleu du casque, vivre d'une vie étrange. L'homme n'a pas les traits puissants de tant d'autres noirs, ni leur carrure, ni leur apparence de force massive et brutale: il est souple, léger, habile sans doute à toutes les ruses. Il a toujours vécu sous le soleil écrasant de Djibouti, au bord d'une mer qui semblait rouler du feu, il a vécu là comme un lézard sur un rocher, inerte d'apparence, mais prompt à la défensive, preste quand vient le danger. Aux portes du désert, dans l'un de ces bastions dont la France jalonne ses routes lointaines, il a toujours vu flotter nos couleurs sur le bleu implacable du ciel. Il les a suives sous la grisaille de nos climats, sous la neige et sous la pluie. Son visage de bronze s'est crispé au grand vent des obus, mais son sang guerrier n'a pas frémi, non plus que n'a vacillé sa fidélité à nos armes.

— 19 —

©Forgotten Heroes 14-19 Limited

Somalia

*The English translation is based on the original notes from the artist, written between 1915 and 1919 and even if some testimonies may sound awkward for people today, the painter was in full admiration of the men he painted and meant no offence in any way.

Morocco

Moroccan Rifleman
Mohamed Ben Bidouan (from Casablanca)

The renowned "MD", the Moroccan Division, has won lanyards of different colors on all the battlefields: it was the first to bathe its colors in the sacred waters of the Rhine. Its soldiers, who came so recently under our command, have proved that they yielded to none in heroism and fidelity. Under their helmet they showed impetuous valor, under their traditional fez they remained splendid. They came from all quarters of Morocco, from the ports on the coast, from enchanting Rabat, from "Marrakech under the palm trees," from the plateaus, from the mountains, from the grim ramparts of Fez. They all brought the same eagerness to fight, the same warlike vigor animated their hearts and fired their muscles. They were on the Marne, in front of Mondement in flames; at Saint-Gout when all seemed lost they won the battle; they were at Verdun, on the Somme, at the Chemin des Dames; they halted the enemy at Chateau-Thierry, then forcibly chased them out of our country. They gave France the utmost service, they remain Moroccans, but they are also Frenchmen.*

La fameuse D.M. a gagné sur tous les champs de bataille les fourragères de coulteurs diverses: la première, elle a baigné ses fanions aux eaux sacrées du Rhin. Ses soldats, depuis si peu de temps sous notre influence, ont montré qu'ils ne le cédaient à personne en héroïsme et en fidélité. Sous le casque ils étaient d'une impétueuse vaillance, sous le faz rituel ils restaient majestueux. Ils étaient venus de toutes les parties du Maroc, des ports de la côte, de Rabat l'enchanteresse, de "Marrakech sous les palmes," des plateaux, de la montagne, des farouches murailles de Fez. Tous ils apportaient la même ardeur à combattre, la même sève guerrière animait leur coeur, actionnait leurs muscles. Ils étaient à la Marne, devant Mondement en flammes, quand à Saint-Gond tout semblait perdu, et ils ont gagné la bataille: ils étaient à Verdun, sur la Somme, au Chemin des Dames: ils ont arrêté l'ennemi à Château Thierry, et l'ont ensuite, à grands coups, bouté hors de chez nous. Ils ont servi la France autant qu'il était possible de le faire: ils restent Marocains, mais ils sont Français.

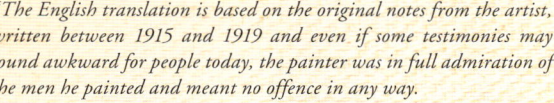

The English translation is based on the original notes from the artist, written between 1915 and 1919 and even if some testimonies may sound awkward for people today, the painter was in full admiration of the men he painted and meant no offence in any way.

India

Eugene Burnand

Roshan Dean (from Cambelpoor, Addock)
Indian army soldier (Muslim)

From the enormous turban emerges a small point: it is the sign of the believer. The man is a Muslim, and there is an air of a dervish, the calm and patient expression, like the imprint of fatalism. We think about a mysterious India, the India of which no one can know all the feelings, all the hopes, all the secrets, the India of enormous forests, of rivers resembling seas, of impenetrable jungle. Warlike tribes, pastoral tribes, village people, country people, people from mountains lost in the sky, submitting to the teachings of the elders, Brahmin or Marabout, a people thoroughly crisscrossed with groups of various beliefs, a people difficult to fathom, to lead towards a definite goal, inexhaustible reservoir of life force, where England knew to find loyal soldiers, always ready to shed the purest of their blood.*

Du turban énorme, émerge une petite pointe: c'est l'insigne du croyant. L'homme est donc mahométan, et il a, en effet, l'air d'un derviche, l'expression patiente et calme, comme empreinte de fatalisme. Nous songeons à l'Inde mystérieuse, l'Inde dont nul ne peut connaître tous les sentiments, toutes les espérances, tous les secrets, l'Inde des forêts énormes, des fleuves semblables à des mers, de la jungle impénétrable. Tribus guerrières, tribus pastorales, peuples des villes, des campagnes, des montagnes perdues dans le ciel, dociles à la parole des sages, brahmanes ou marabouts, population grouillante traversée de grands mouvements d'opinion, population malaisée à orienter, à mener vers un but défini, réservoir inépuisable de forces et de vie, où l'Angleterre a su cependant, trouver des soldats loyaux, toujours prêts a donner pour elle le plus pur de son sang.

*The English translation is based on the original notes from the artist, written between 1915 and 1919 and even if some testimonies may sound awkward for people today, the painter was in full admiration of the men he painted and meant no offence in any way.

Islam

1. It is forbidden in Islam to issue fatwas without the necessary training. Even then fatwas must follow Islamic legal theory as defined in the classical texts. It is also forbidden to cite a portion of a verse from the Qur'an—or part of a verse—to derive a ruling without looking at everything that the Qur'an and Hadith have to say on that particular matter. In other words, there are strict subjective and objective prerequisites for issuing fatwas, and one cannot "cherry-pick" Qur'anic verses for legal arguments without considering the entire corpus of Qur'an and Hadith literature.

2. It is forbidden in Islam to issue legal rulings about anything without mastery of the Arabic language. The Mufti (Muslim legal scholar) also needs to be proficiently versed in the Qur'an and Hadith as well as the various other disciplines such as osool ul fiq (fundamentals of jurisprudence).

3. It is forbidden in Islam to oversimplify Shari'ah matters and ignore established Islamic sciences.

4. It is permissible in Islam [for scholars] to differ on any matter, except for the fundamental tenants of faith such as the five pillars that all Muslims must know.

5. When deriving legal rulings in Islam, it is forbidden to ignore the reality of contemporary times and the circumstances or context in which a person may be living.

6. It is forbidden in Islam to kill the innocent.

7. It is forbidden to kill livestock, destroy farmland and when engaged in warfare to harm non combatants.

8. It is forbidden in Islam to kill emissaries, ambassadors, and diplomats; hence it is forbidden to kill journalists and aid workers.

9. Jihad in Islam is a broad term that transcends warfare. Military jihad is traditionally defensive and has a number of prerequisites. It is not permissible to engage in jihad without due cause or without following strict prescribed guidelines. At its heart, jihad means to struggle and there are many forms. Controlling one's desires and self (jihad al-nafs) is considered among the most praiseworthy forms of jihad.

10. It is forbidden in Islam to declare a person a disbeliever unless he (or she) openly declares disbelief.

11. Islam refers to the Jews and Christians as "ahlul-kitaab" (People of the Book) and acknowledges both religions as being revelations from God.

12. Islam acknowledges all of the prophets mentioned in the Old and New Testaments, including Adam, Noah, Abraham, Moses and Jesus.

13. Islam acknowledges the original Old Testament (Hebrew, Torah) and the original New Testament (Christian, Injeel) as scriptures sent down by God.

14. Islam acknowledges the Prophet Abraham as the father of modern monotheistic religion.

15. It is forbidden in Islam to harm or mistreat—in any way—Christians, Jews or any other people without due cause.

16. The re-introduction of slavery is forbidden in Islam. It was abolished by universal consensus.

17. It is forbidden in Islam to force people to convert or force them to abandon their faiths.

18. It is forbidden in Islam to deny women their rights.

19. It is forbidden in Islam to deny children their rights.

20. It is forbidden in Islam to enact legal punishments (hudud) without following the correct procedures that ensure justice and mercy.

21. It is forbidden in Islam to torture people.

22. It is forbidden in Islam to disfigure the dead.

23. It is forbidden in Islam to attribute evil acts to God.

24. It is forbidden in Islam to destroy the graves and shrines of Prophets and Companions.

25. Armed insurrection against the government is forbidden in Islam for any reason other than clear disbelief by the ruler and not allowing people to pray.

26. It is forbidden in Islam to declare a caliphate without the consensus of all Muslims.

27. Loyalty to one's nation is permissible in Islam but is not permissible over loyalty to the religion or the Muslim community.

28. After the death of the Prophet, Islam does not require anyone to emigrate anywhere.

This letter, signed by more than 100 Muslim scholars from around the world was published in September 2014
http://www.lettertobaghdadi.com/
http://lettertobaghdadi.com/14/english-v14.pdf

> *None of us knows what might happen even the next minute, yet still we go forward.*
> *Because we trust.*
> *Because we have Faith.*

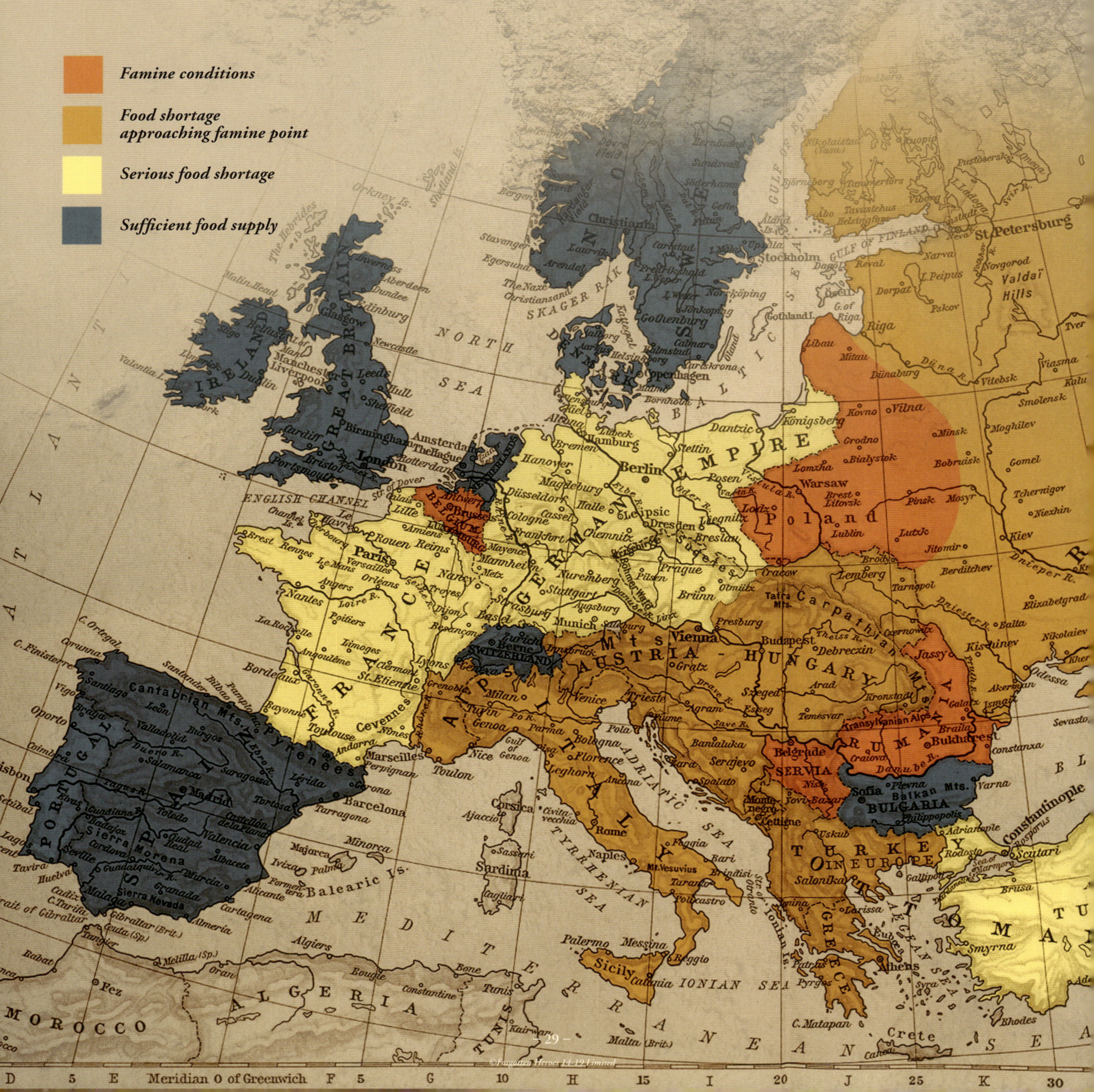

Civilian deaths in France: 500,000*
300,000 - military operations and food shortages.
200,000 - Spanish Flu.

Civilian deaths in Belgium: 92,000*
62,000 - food shortages and German reprisals.
30,000 - Spanish Flu.

Reports and letters mention that Muslim soldiers shared their food with the local people who were suffering from famine in Europe. This, despite the fact that they knew it would weaken their own strength, needed for the fierce fights to come.

> The Prophet was asked:
> "Which charity is best?"
> He replied,
> "That which you give while you fear poverty."
> Sahih Bukhari 500

*http://www.centre-robert-schuman.org

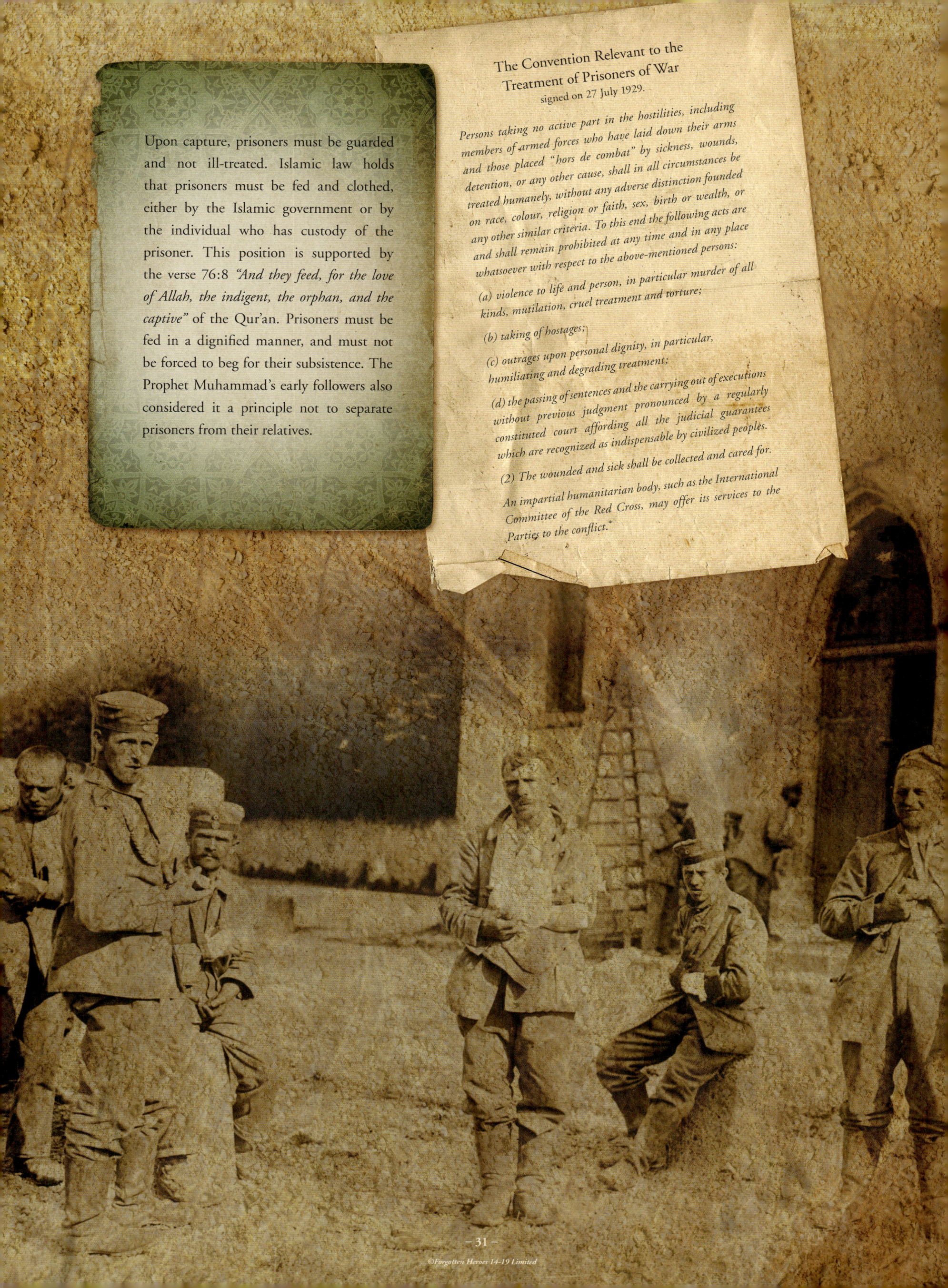

Upon capture, prisoners must be guarded and not ill-treated. Islamic law holds that prisoners must be fed and clothed, either by the Islamic government or by the individual who has custody of the prisoner. This position is supported by the verse 76:8 *"And they feed, for the love of Allah, the indigent, the orphan, and the captive"* of the Qur'an. Prisoners must be fed in a dignified manner, and must not be forced to beg for their subsistence. The Prophet Muhammad's early followers also considered it a principle not to separate prisoners from their relatives.

The Convention Relevant to the Treatment of Prisoners of War
signed on 27 July 1929.

Persons taking no active part in the hostilities, including members of armed forces who have laid down their arms and those placed "hors de combat" by sickness, wounds, detention, or any other cause, shall in all circumstances be treated humanely, without any adverse distinction founded on race, colour, religion or faith, sex, birth or wealth, or any other similar criteria. To this end the following acts are and shall remain prohibited at any time and in any place whatsoever with respect to the above-mentioned persons:

(a) violence to life and person, in particular murder of all kinds, mutilation, cruel treatment and torture;

(b) taking of hostages;

(c) outrages upon personal dignity, in particular, humiliating and degrading treatment;

(d) the passing of sentences and the carrying out of executions without previous judgment pronounced by a regularly constituted court affording all the judicial guarantees which are recognized as indispensable by civilized peoples.

(2) The wounded and sick shall be collected and cared for. An impartial humanitarian body, such as the International Committee of the Red Cross, may offer its services to the Parties to the conflict.

Officers were surprised when Muslim soldiers lectured them about the fact that captured prisoners of war should be taken to a place that had been prepared for them, they should not harm them or torture them with beatings, deprive them of food and water, leave them out in the sun or the cold, burn them with fire, or put covers over their mouths, ears and eyes and put them in cages like animals. Rather they should treat them with kindness and mercy and feed them well.*

Compassion is the basis of morality.

*http://www.refworld.org/docid/3ae6b36c8.html
https://www.icrc.org/eng/war-and-law/protected-persons/prisoners-war/overview-detainees-protected-persons.htm

For most Muslims around the world, the month of Ramadan marks a yearly renewal, a time to turn inward in spiritual reflection, upward to God in worship, and outward toward other human beings in acts of charity. It is a time when many Muslims, who do not offer the five required daily prayers or have much to do with religion for the rest of the year, refrain from food and drink during the daylight hours of an entire lunar month for the sake of God. Among the five pillars of Islam it is the fast of Ramadan that is the most universally observed Muslim practice worldwide, behind only belief in God and the Prophet Muhammad.

Eid al-Fitr *"feast of breaking the fast"* is an important religious holiday that marks the end of Ramadan.

> *May the magic of Eid bring lots of happiness in your life and may you celebrate it with all your close friends & may it fill your heart with wonders.*

War circumstances allowed Muslim soldiers to be relieved of their religious obligations in order to preserve their lives. But for some soldiers such choices were complicated by the fact that they faced trying conditions in the trenches. For many, religious observance was crucial for coping with the hardship and challenges of the battlefront.

The army supplied Muslims with adequate food, whenever possible. An Indian soldier (Hemayat Ullah Khan) wrote on 6 August 1916 to his Imam in Hindustan, *"However heavy may be the firing, whether of shells or bullets or both, fresh goat's flesh and dal and cakes of various kinds with gur (half-refined sugar) and tea reach the trenches of the Indians without fail. The entire force is very pleased with these arrangements."*

> Don't walk in front of me
> I may not follow
> Don't walk behind me
> I may not lead
> Walk beside me
> just be my friend
>
> — Albert Camus

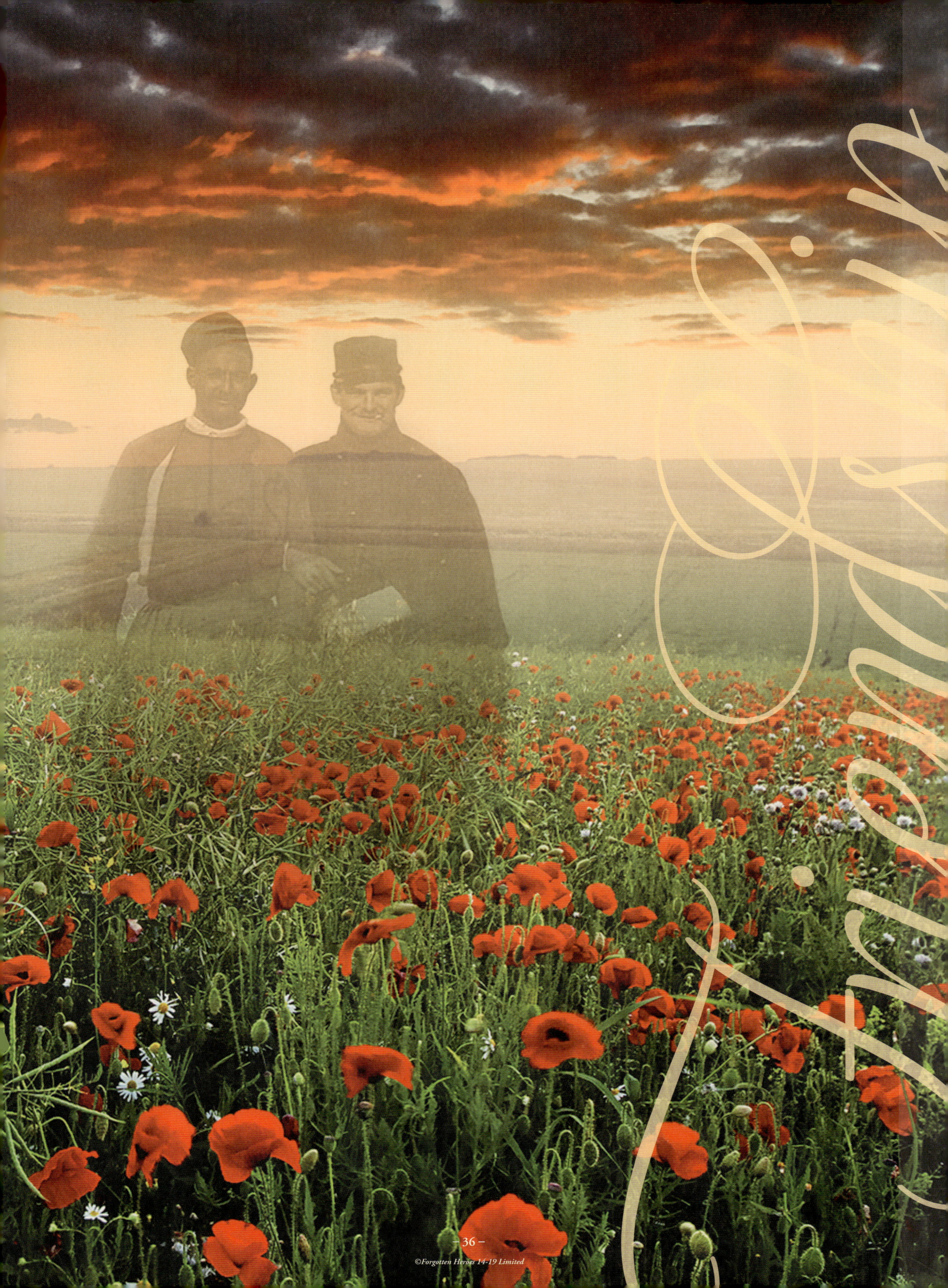

©Forgotten Heroes 14-19 Limited

Various documents mention Muslim soldiers sharing their native cultural medical knowledge with nurses and doctors at the battlefront who had run out of medical supplies.

The war produced medical issues largely unknown in civilian life and not previously experienced by doctors or nurses. Most common were wound infections, contracted when men riddled by machine gun bullets had bits of uniform and the polluted mud of the trenches driven into their abdomens and internal organs.

> *I think…if it is true that there are as many minds as there are heads, then there are as many kinds of love as there are hearts.*
>
> Leo Tolstoy

Charlotte Béatrice de Rothschild (14 September 1864 – 7 April 1934) was a member of the prominent Rothschild banking family of France and offered her villa in Paris to be used as a hospital for all wounded soldiers no matter their cultural or religious background, including Muslims.

– 38 –

©Forgotten Heroes 14-19 Limited

> If I can see pain in your eyes,
> share with me your tears.
> If I can see joy in your eyes then
> share with me your smile.

Musulmans.
N° 6. R.

Hôpital Temporaire N° 31.

Rapport hebdomadaire

> *I don't want to be rich. I want to die knowing I stood in front of a broken soldier and gave him a reason to smile again.*

algériens	tunisiens	marocains	sénégalais	
94	18	15	5	

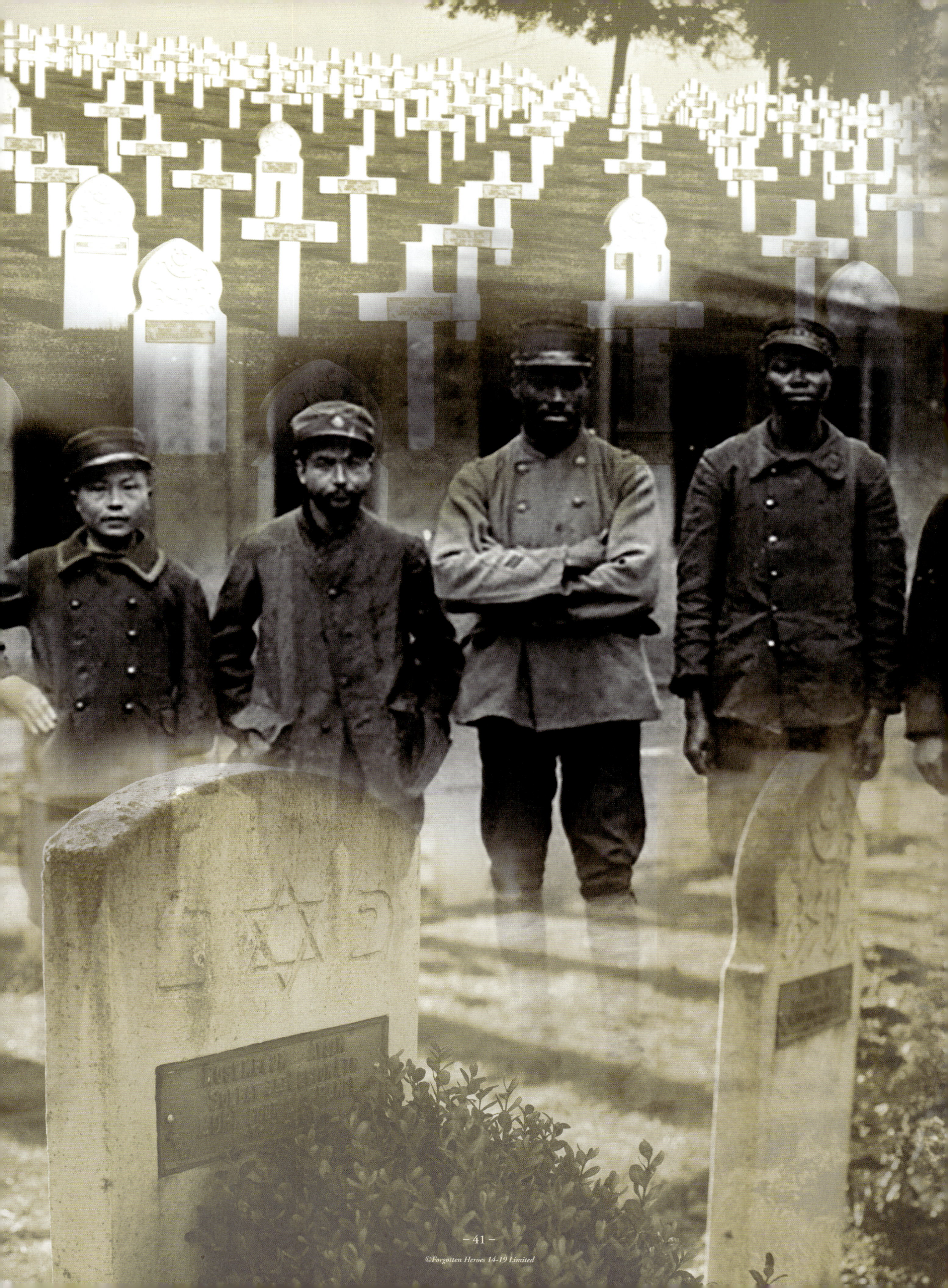

©Forgotten Heroes 14-19 Limited

It's time for parents to teach young people early on that in diversity there is beauty and there is strength.

> *If we cannot end now our differences, at least we can help make the world safe for diversity.*
>
> John F. Kennedy

Diversity

> Our most basic common link is
> that we all inhabit this small planet.
> We all breathe the same air.
> We all cherish our children's future.
> And we are all mortal.
>
> John F. Kennedy

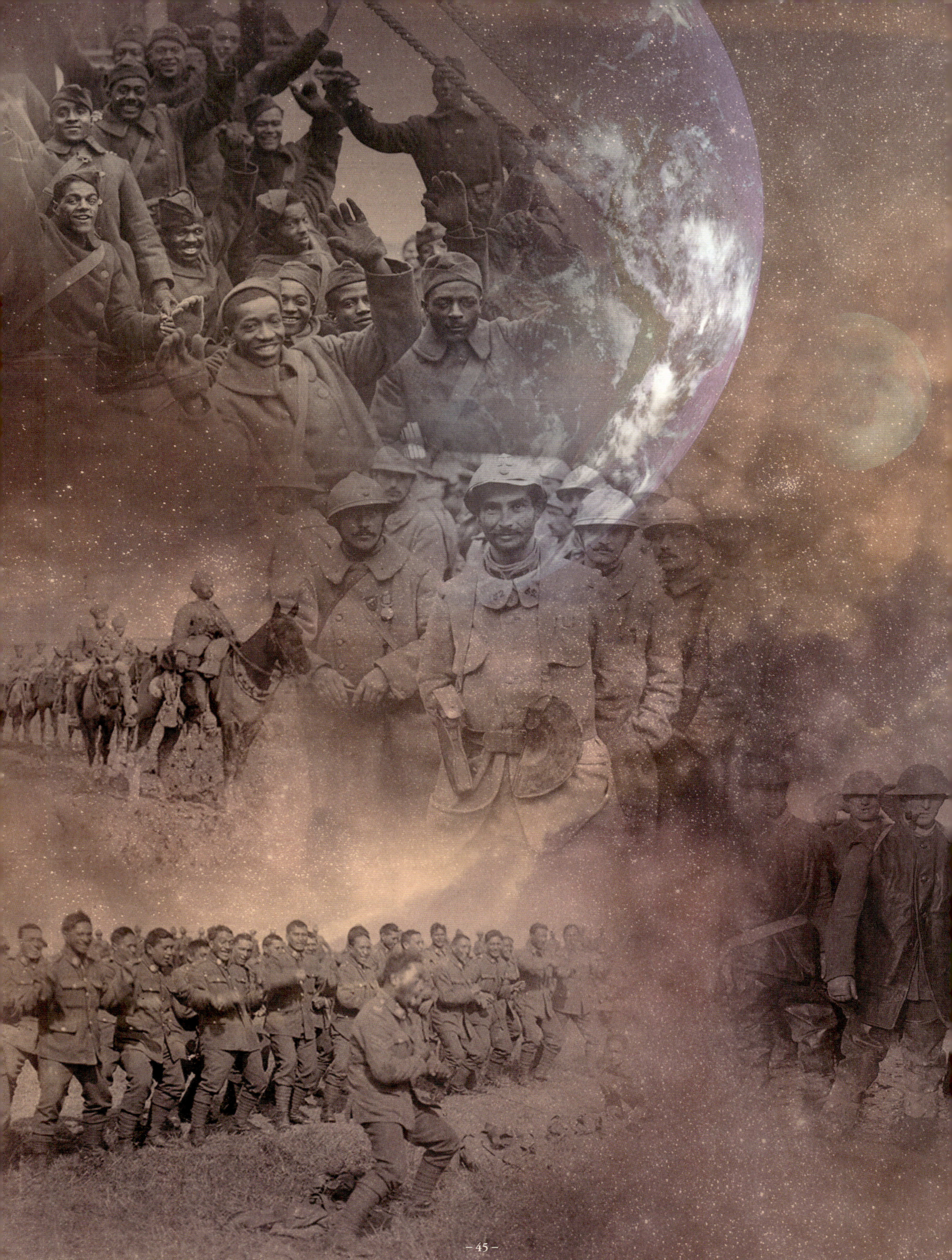

©Forgotten Heroes 14-19 Limited

> *The greatness of humanity
> is not in being human,
> but in being humane.*
>
> Mahatma Gandhi

Don't envy my smile because it took me a lot of tears to get it. When you see Glory, ask for the Story.

Ring of Remembrance, Notre-Dame de Lorette, France

The Fallen

They shall grow not old, as we that are left grow old:
Age shall not weary them, nor the years condemn.
At the going down of the sun and in the morning
We will remember them.

They went with songs to the battle, they were young,
Straight of limb, true of eye, steady and aglow.
They were staunch to the end against odds uncounted,
They fell with their faces to the foe.

Tears are words the heart can't say.

Robert Laurence Binyon (1869-1943)

Australian War Memorial, Canberra, Australia

A Trio of Brave English Soldiers who Joined the Colors of Islam
From left to right: Gunner F Leadon (Azeez*), Pte Ballard (Mubarak*), Gunner H Camp (Basheer*)

*Muslim name

> God will not look you over for medals or degrees but for scars.

British India sent around 1,5 million men (of these around 400,000 were Muslims) to nearly all theatres of war across Europe, Africa and Asia. Units were composed of soldiers from various ethnic groups or classes, mainly Sikhs, Punjabi Muslims, Punjabi Hindus, Brahmins and Rajputs.

> I cannot teach
> anybody anything.
> I can only
> make them think.
> — Socrates

Neuve-Chapelle Indian Memorial, France

> One cannot and must not try to erase the Allied Muslim contribution during World War 1 merely because it does not fit the present.

الخطوط الأولى فوق الخنادق المغتصبة

December 1916

We live in caves like hedgehogs and we constantly have rain on our heads; we are exposed to deafening noises, peoples' faces change and are altered under the effect of fear; we are in a state that language cannot describe. This country has been forsaken by Allah.

Meat is brought to us in dishes but we don't know whether it is permitted or prohibited; this is a source of torment for me. I think about it day and night and you must tell me how I stand now in relation to Allah. Let me tell you, my dear father, and I swear by Allah and by that which we hold sacred, I will never stop saying my prayers. I will never abandon my faith even if I am assailed by ordeals more terrible than those in which I find myself. I am not boasting when I speak like this; I am inspired by Allah. I ask Him to help me to remain true to Him and to save me.

Letter from an unknown Algerian soldier

مشاة فرنسا

> *These documents will foster a new found pride & confidence among Muslim youth by affirming their strong, positive religious identity in Europe.*
> Hayyan Ayaz Bhabha

The French War Minister Alexandre Millerand who had a great respect for Muslims instructed all soldiers to comply with following instructions.

=======

Rules to be followed for the burial of the Muslim military

=======

The desire to be buried according to the rites of religion and Muslim customs, which seem to be of the highest concern to the native soldiers who come to die in France, as well as their families, I believe it is useful to supplement the instructions I gave you by dispatch No. 4695-9/11 of 16 October last, indicating all the formalities that accompany the death of a Muslim and specifying those that I think can be put into practise.

When a Muslim is about to die, he will always, when he can, pronounce the "Chehada" setting the index of the right hand or holding the Qur'an. If his state does not allow him to do so himself, anybody present is obliged to help him and pronounce for him this profession of Muslim faith "I bear witness that there is no God but Allah, and I bear witness that Muhammad is the Messenger of Allah."

As death has done its work, the body is completely washed in hot water. The body wrapped in a shroud, which consists of a white cotton blanket wide enough to completely surround the deceased, is then transported instead of burial on a stretcher covered with a cloth... Putting in a coffin is absolutely forbidden.

The tomb must be dug with a southwest-northeast orientation, so that, with the body being placed on the right side, the face is turned in the direction of Mecca.

This practice is feasible and it will be necessary to comply with it.

Finally, it would be desirable that, by analogy with what is done for Christians, whose tomb is usually surmounted by a cross, the tombs of the Muslim military are marked by means of two stones or wooden steles, of which the model is attached, and which will be placed: one above the place where the head rests, bearing the inscription in Arabic (conforming to the model) that it will be easy to copy and the name of the deceased in French, the other without inscription, at the location of the feet.

This memory that we owe to our dead Muslim soldiers for France is easily achievable.

RÉPUBLIQUE FRANÇAISE

Direction du Service de Santé

2° Bureau

Matériel - Établissements du Service de Santé

Règles à suivre pour l'inhumation des militaires musulmans .

N° 11.282-2/7

Bordeaux le 3 Décembre 1914

LE MINISTRE DE LA GUERRE

à Monsieur le Général Commandant la Région du Nord

à Boulogne sur mer

Le souci d'être inhumés suivant les rites consacrés par la religion et les usages musulmans paraissant préoccuper au plus haut point les militaires indigénes qui viennent à décéder en France, ainsi que leurs familles, je crois utile de compléter les instructions que je vous ai données, par dépêche N° 4695-9/11 du 16 Octobre dernier en vous indiquant toutes les formalités qui accompagnent le décés d'un musulman et en précisant celles qui me paraissent pouvoir être mises en pratique .

Lorsqu'un musulman est sur le point de mourir, il ne manque pas, lorsqu'il le peut, de prononcer la " Chehada " en dressant l'index de la main droite. si son état ne lui permet pas de le faire lui-même, tout coreligionnaire présent est dans l'obligation de prononcer pour lui cette profession de foi musulmane .

Il y aura donc lieu, chaque fois qu'un militaire indigéne sera dans un état désespéré, de prévenir le ou les coreligionnaires qui pourront se trouver dans le même établissement que lui .

La mort ayant fait son oeuvre, le corps est entiérement lavé à l'eau chaude .

Cette pratique ne me parait pas applicable ailleurs qu'en pays musulman, car les indigénes répugnent à cette besogne, la confiant dans chaque agglomération à un professionnel. Il n'apparait donc pas que les coreligionnaires du défunt présents dans les hopitaux, s'en chargeraient volontiers; mais s'ils en témoignaient le désir, toutes facilités devraient leur être données à ce sujet .

Le corps enveloppé dans un linceul, qui consiste en une cotonnade blanche quelconque assez large pour entourer complétement le défunt, est ensuite transporté au lieu d'inhumation sur une civiére recouverte d'une étoffe qui pourrait être tricolore . La civiére doit être portée à bras par des coreligionnaires la mise dans un cercueil est absolument interdite .

La cérémonie qui accompagne les funérailles, ne peut être dirigée que par un musulman, en ce qui concerne le rite religieux, car lui seul a qualité pour dire les prières . Il conviendra donc d'en charger le ou les camarades du défunt tout en rendant, bien entendu, les honneurs militaires en usage .

En cas d'absence de tout musulman, les honneurs militaires seuls seront accordés et on devra s'abstenir de toute cérémonie ayant un caractère religieux, comme je l'ai déjà prescrit par dépêche N° 4695-9/11 précitée .

La tombe doit être creusée avec une orientation sud-ouest nord est, de façon que, le corps étant placé du coté droit, le visage soit tourné dans la direction de La Mecque .

Cette pratique est réalisable et il y aura lieu de s'y conformer .

Enfin, il serait désirable que, par analogie avec ce qui se fait pour les chrétiens, dont la tombe est habituellement surmontée d'une croix, les tombes ~~xxxxxxxxxxxxxxxxxx~~ des militaires musulmans fussent marqués au moyen de deux stéles en

pierre ou en ....

en pierre ou en bois, dont le modéle est ci-joint, et qui seront placées: l'une au dessus de l'endroit ou repose la tête, portant l'inscription en arabe (conforme au modéle) qu'il sera facile de faire recopier et le nom du défunt en Français, l'autre sans inscription, à l'emplacement des pieds .

Ce souvenir que nous devons a nos soldats musulmans morts pour la France est facilement réalisable .

Vous voudrez bien communiquer ces instructions aux Médecins Chefs des hôpitaux militaires et auxiliaires , ainsi qu'aux Commandants de dépots de convalescents et des dépots des troupes d'Afrique placées sous votre commandement en leur recommandant de s'y conformer dans toute la mesure du possible .

Signé: MILLERAND .

Pour Copie conforme
Le Général de Division Bautdemoulin
Commandant la Région du Nord
P.O. le Chef d'Etat-Major
Boulogne sur mer le 10 Avril 1915

M. La Salle

Stéle en bois découpé d'après le modéle ci-joint, peinte en blanc – Inscriptions et croissant en noir.

Tête

Pieds

Nom du Mort
N° de son Régiment
Date
en français

Stéle de même forme que la précédente sans inscriptions avec simplement l'étoile et le croissant.

©Forgotten Heroes 14-19 Limited

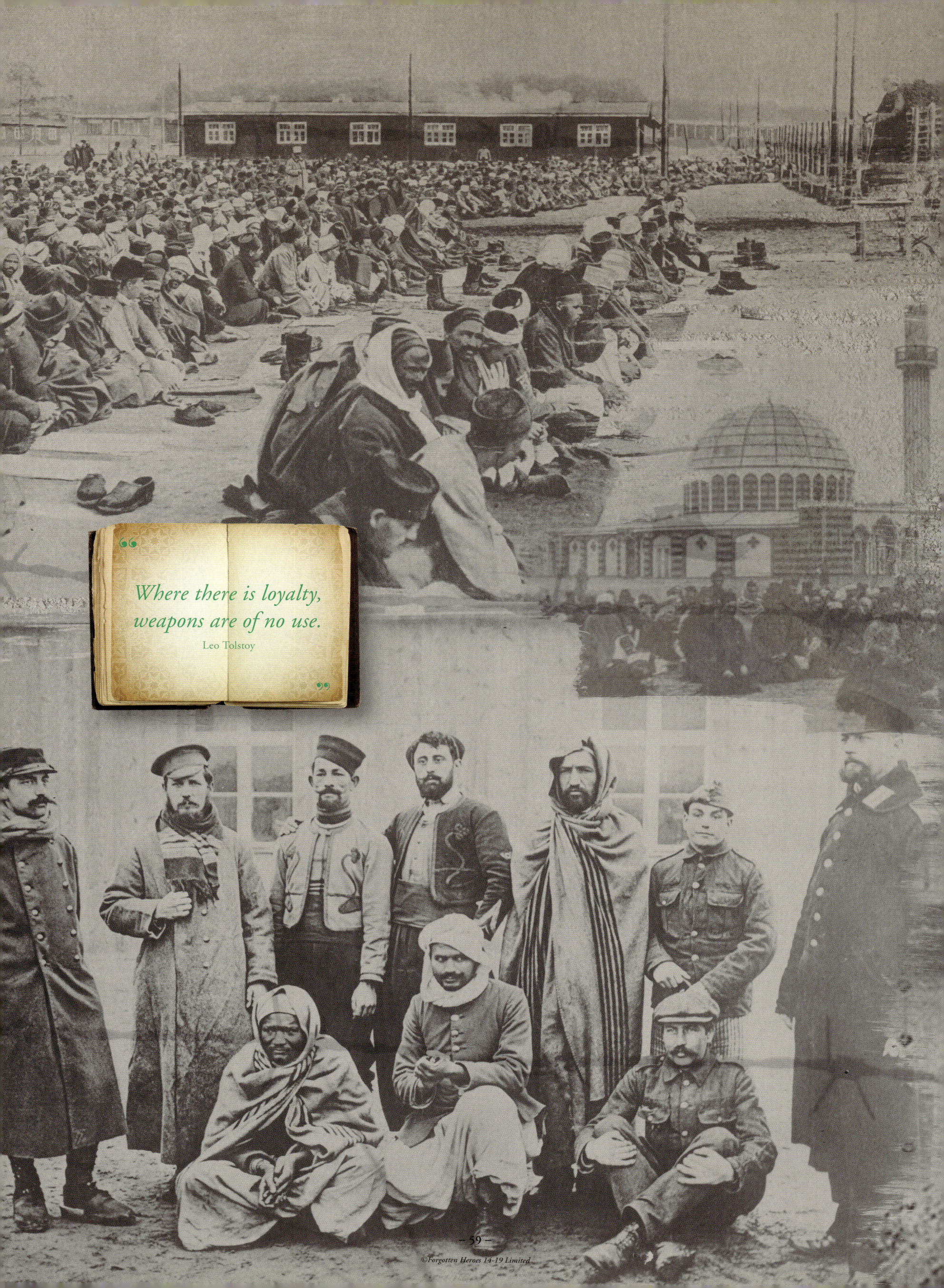

> *Where there is loyalty, weapons are of no use.*
> Leo Tolstoy

Halbmondlager (known in English as the *"Half Moon Camp"*) was a prisoner of war camp in Wünsdorf Germany, for Muslims only. It was the site of the first mosque ever to be built in Germany, a large and ornate wooden structure finished in July 1915. The camp housed approximately 30,000 Muslim prisoners who had fought for the Allied side. (Gerhard Höpp[*])

The intended and sole purpose of the camp was to convince Muslim prisoners of war to wage jihad against the United Kingdom, France and Russia. There is little information about how many Muslims joined the Ottoman army to fight against their colonial masters, except that they were very few.

[*]*Muslime in der Mark. Als Kriegsgefangene und Internierte in Wünsdorf und Zossen, 1914–1924.*

The first major gas attack occurred on 22 April 1915.

The Moroccan and Algerian troops in the path of the gas cloud sustained about 6,000 casualties on the spot. Most Muslims, along with others affected, died within ten minutes (primarily from asphyxia and tissue damage to the lungs), and many more were blinded.

> *I have accepted fear as part of my life.*
> *I have gone ahead despite the pounding in the heart that says:*
>
> *Turn back...*

Anthony R Hossack of Queen Victoria's Rifles described the chaos as the French Colonial Corps troops fled from the gas, *"Plainly something terrible was happening. What was it? Officers, and Staff officers too, stood gazing at the scene, awestruck and dumbfounded; for in the northerly breeze there came a pungent nauseating smell that tickled the throat and made our eyes smart. The horses and men were still pouring down the road. Two or three men on a horse, I saw, while over the fields streamed mobs of infantry, the dusky warriors of French Africa; away went their rifles, equipment, even their tunics that they might run the faster. One man came stumbling through our lines. An officer of ours held him up with levelled revolver, 'What's the matter, you bloody lot of cowards?' he says. The Zouave was frothing at the mouth, his eyes started from their sockets, and he fell writhing at the officer's feet."*

Battle of the Marne

The Moroccan Division was one of the most decorated units of the French Army and all its regiments were cited in the orders of the armed forces at the end of the conflict. The Moroccan Division was the only French division to be decorated with the légion d'honneur during the course of World War I.

Exhausted by their sea trip from Morocco on 10 August 1914, the Moroccan Division was quickly given new uniforms: *"khaki clothes with trousers buckled with large red belts; they wore a red chechia hidden under a khaki turban."*

By 4 September 1914 they were engaged on the battlefield in an area of Ile-de-France. One of the major French military figures, Marechal Juin, who took part in the fighting, would later write, *"regardless of the difficult experiences, both moral and physical, never have the Moroccans shown to be more confident than on this day of September 5th, which was a prelude to the big battle of Marne, where these soldiers stopped the German advance."*

It was immediately called *"the miracle of the Marne"* as without the enormous sacrifice of these mainly Muslim soldiers, Paris would probably have been captured by the German troops. Only 800 of the 4,200 Moroccan soldiers survived the battle of the Marne.

> *I could hear my heart beating. I could hear everyone's heart beating. Not one of us is moving, not even when the trenches went dark.*
>
> From the diary of an unknown soldier

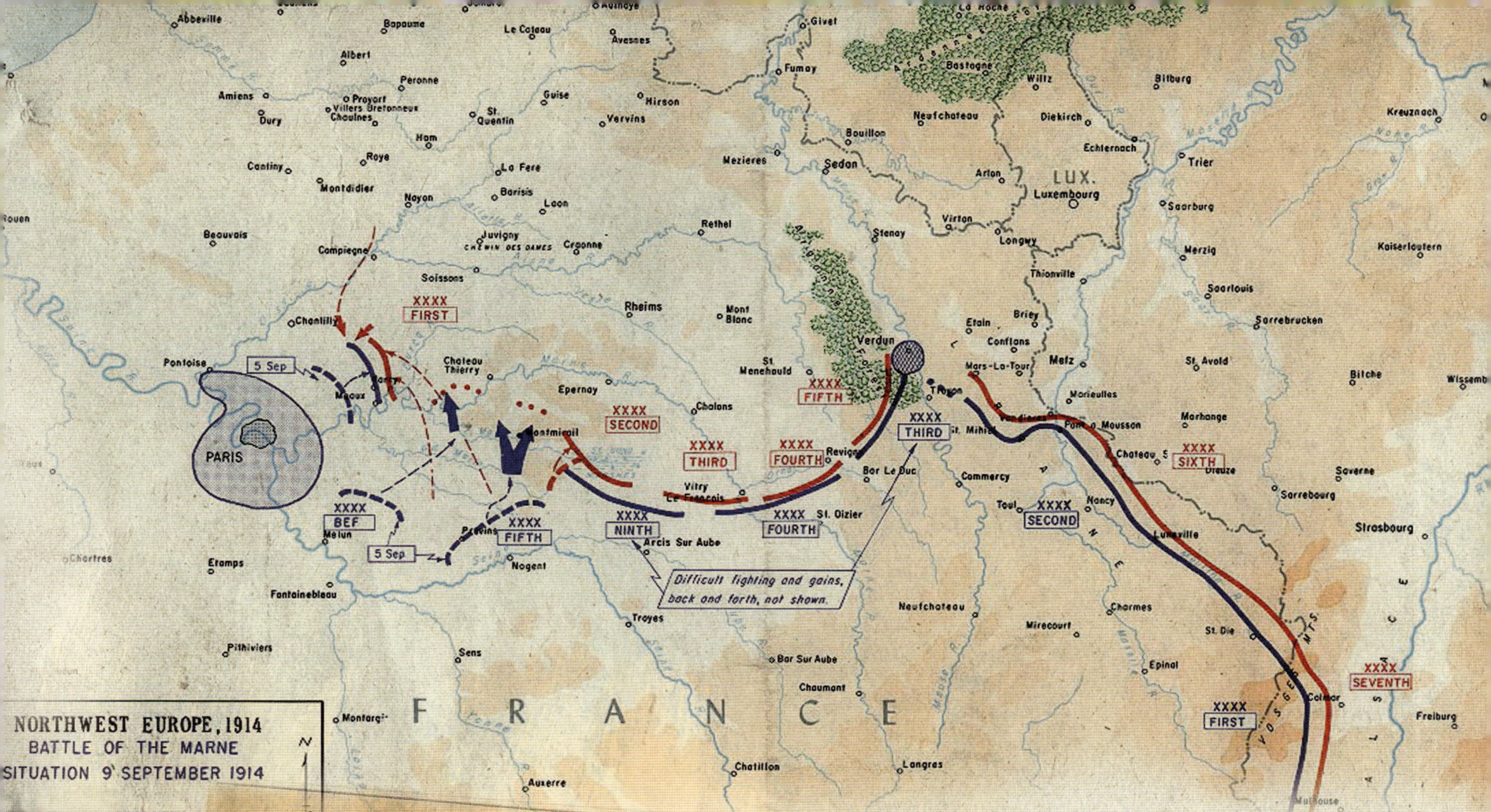

NORTHWEST EUROPE, 1914
BATTLE OF THE MARNE
SITUATION 9ᵗʰ SEPTEMBER 1914

A LA BRIGADE MAROCAINE

Dédié au colonel P...

Penchard et Neufmontiers, lieux à jamais célèbres,
Collines et vallons, que septembre dorait,
Vous gardez maintenant sous vos tertres funèbres
Des héros que la soif de vaincre dévorait.

Je vous revois encor, braves entre les braves,
Ignorant les abris, les terriers, les couverts,
Franchir les fils de fer, mépriser leurs entraves
Et vous ruer sur le Boche hypocrite et pervers.

Il vous faut peu de temps pour culbuter leur ligne.
Malgré le feu barrant, rapide et meurtrier,
Vous traversez le Rû. Neufmontiers, sur un signe
De vos valeureux chefs, est repris tout entier.

Mais le bois de Penchard cache des mitrailleuses,
Qui sèment en vos rangs le carnage et la mort.
Leur nombre a tôt raison des charges furieuses
Que vous tentez en vain pour conjurer le sort.

Quel est votre devoir ? Tenir coûte que coûte
Ou bien périr sur place, avait dit Maunoury.
Il vous sait résolus, il s'en souvient sans doute
Car il vous a jugés soldats à Barbery.

Que reste-t-il de vous ? ô brigade héroïque!
La mort fauche et refauche encor les plus vaillants.
Les nommer ? Ils sont trop sous ces tombes rustiques
Qui ne prendront plus part aux retours triomphants.

O vous, fils de l'Islam, qui dormez dans la plaine,
Tirailleurs marocains, et chefs européens,
Officiers éprouvés qui mourez à la peine,
La France a reconnu vos efforts surhumains.

Nous serions des ingrats, depuis la Victoire,
Si plus heureux que vous, rentrés dans nos foyers,
Nous ne pensions souvent à chanter votre gloire,
Et couvrir vos tombeaux de fleurs et de lauriers.

Septembre 1916.
L. LOTRON,
ex-sergent mitrailleur, 2ᵉ Régt de tirailleurs indig.
brigade marocaine.

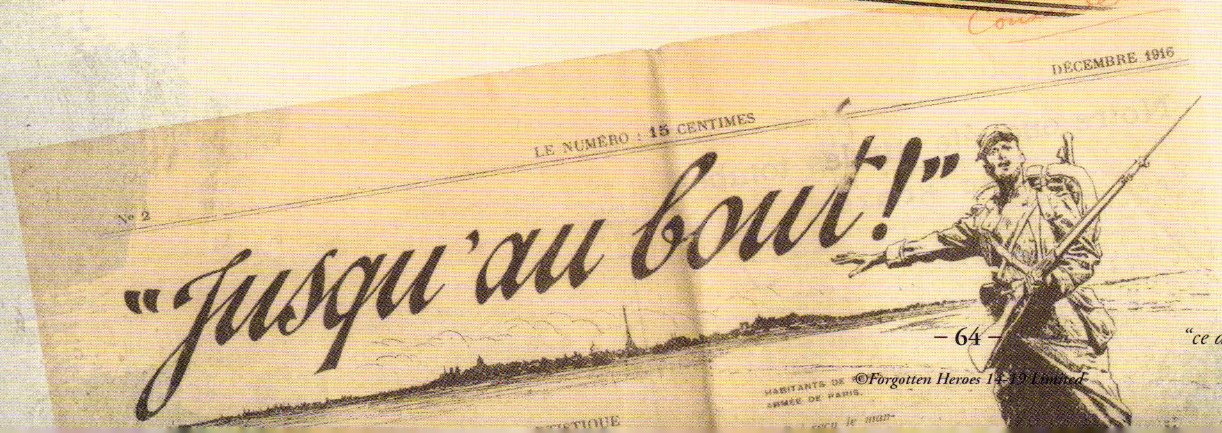

The Moroccan Division

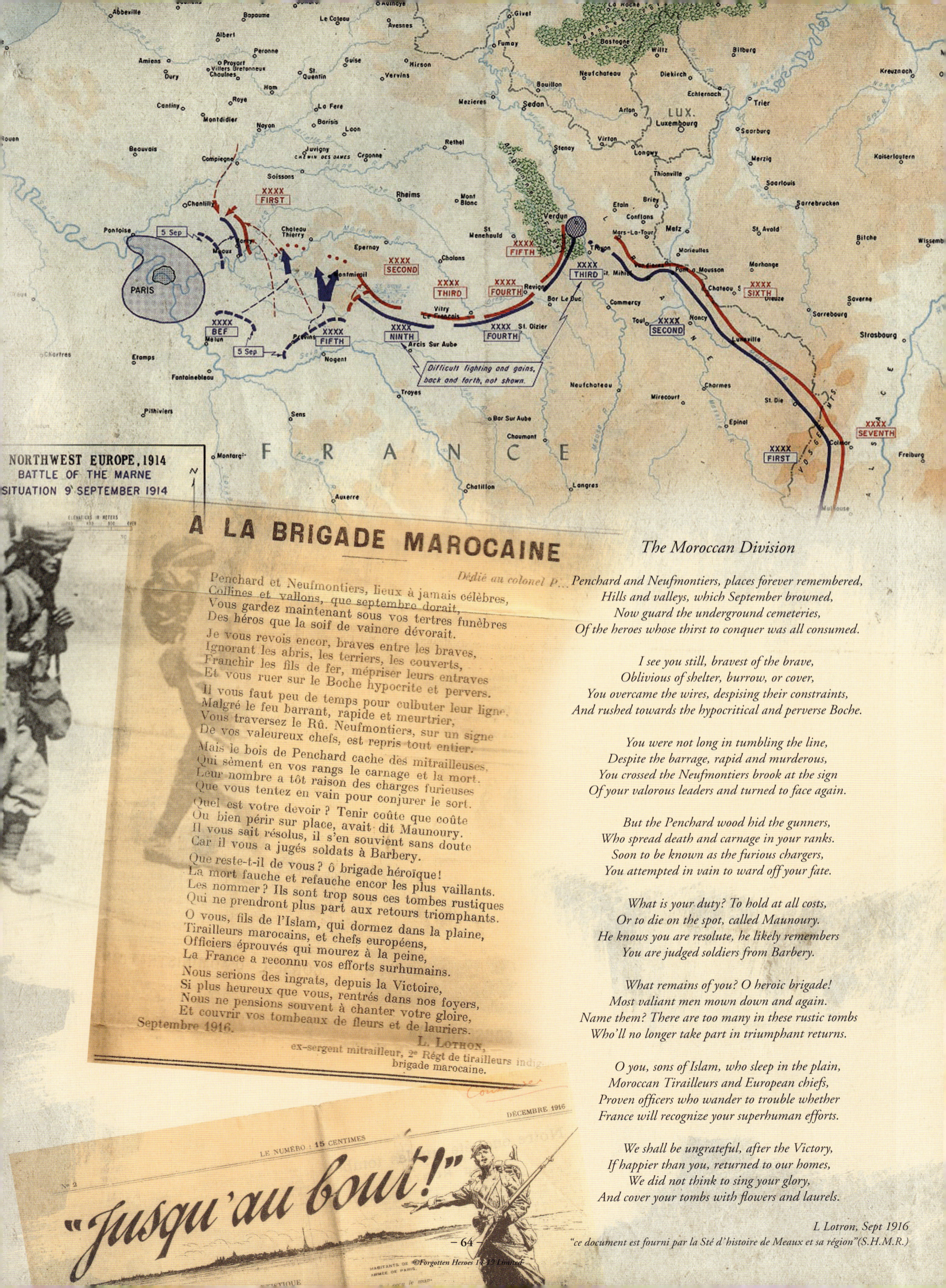

Penchard and Neufmontiers, places forever remembered,
Hills and valleys, which September browned,
Now guard the underground cemeteries,
Of the heroes whose thirst to conquer was all consumed.

I see you still, bravest of the brave,
Oblivious of shelter, burrow, or cover,
You overcame the wires, despising their constraints,
And rushed towards the hypocritical and perverse Boche.

You were not long in tumbling the line,
Despite the barrage, rapid and murderous,
You crossed the Neufmontiers brook at the sign
Of your valorous leaders and turned to face again.

But the Penchard wood hid the gunners,
Who spread death and carnage in your ranks.
Soon to be known as the furious chargers,
You attempted in vain to ward off your fate.

What is your duty? To hold at all costs,
Or to die on the spot, called Maunoury.
He knows you are resolute, he likely remembers
You are judged soldiers from Barbery.

What remains of you? O heroic brigade!
Most valiant men mown down and again.
Name them? There are too many in these rustic tombs
Who'll no longer take part in triumphant returns.

O you, sons of Islam, who sleep in the plain,
Moroccan Tirailleurs and European chiefs,
Proven officers who wander to trouble whether
France will recognize your superhuman efforts.

We shall be ungrateful, after the Victory,
If happier than you, returned to our homes,
We did not think to sing your glory,
And cover your tombs with flowers and laurels.

L Lotron, Sept 1916
"ce document est fourni par la Sté d'histoire de Meaux et sa région"(S.H.M.R.)

"Jusqu'au bout!"
N° 2 — LE NUMÉRO : 15 CENTIMES — DÉCEMBRE 1916

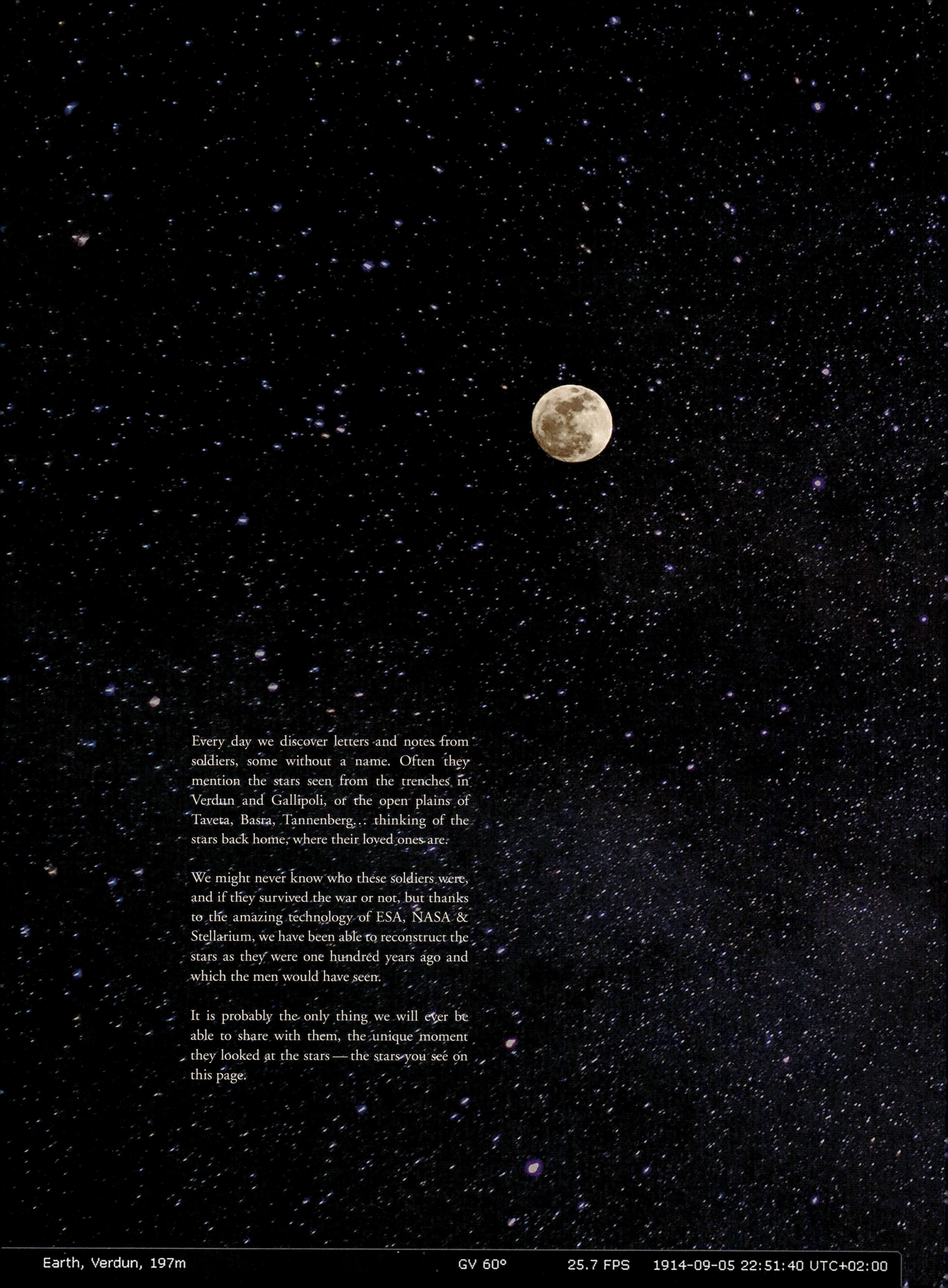

Every day we discover letters and notes from soldiers, some without a name. Often they mention the stars seen from the trenches in Verdun and Gallipoli, or the open plains of Taveta, Basra, Tannenberg... thinking of the stars back home, where their loved ones are.

We might never know who these soldiers were, and if they survived the war or not, but thanks to the amazing technology of ESA, NASA & Stellarium, we have been able to reconstruct the stars as they were one hundred years ago and which the men would have seen.

It is probably the only thing we will ever be able to share with them, the unique moment they looked at the stars — the stars you see on this page.

Earth, Verdun, 197m GV 60° 25.7 FPS 1914-09-05 22:51:40 UTC+02:00

> A sense of the universe, a sense of all,
> the nostalgia which seizes us when
> confronted by nature, beauty, music
> – these seem to be an expectation and
> awareness of a Great Presence.
>
> Pierre Teilhard de Chardin

> *...off the white town hung between the blazing sky and its reflection in the mirage that swept and rolled over the wide lagoon, then the heat of Arabia came out like a drawn sword and struck us speechless.*
>
> T E Lawrence

The Arab Revolt

Before the outbreak of the First World War, challenged by local leaders and Arab nationalists, Ottoman control over the tribes of the Arabian peninsula was relatively weak. In 1916, encouraged by British and French support with promises of independence, Sharif Hussein Ibn Ali staged a revolt in Mecca against Ottoman rule. A British officer, T E Lawrence influenced the Arab rebels who disrupted supplies with raids on the Hejaz railway. The effect of the revolt was to tie down thousands of Ottoman troops who otherwise might have been used to assault British occupied Egypt.

In 1917, the Arab forces successfully occupied the Ottoman held part of Aqaba on the Red Sea coast. Vital Arab intelligence also supported the British conquest of Palestine. After the war, the Hejaz became independent and two Hashemite princes became rulers with British support of what are now Jordan and Iraq. However, the post-war settlement fell far short of Allied promises and much Arab land in effect changed from Ottoman to British or French control as mandates.

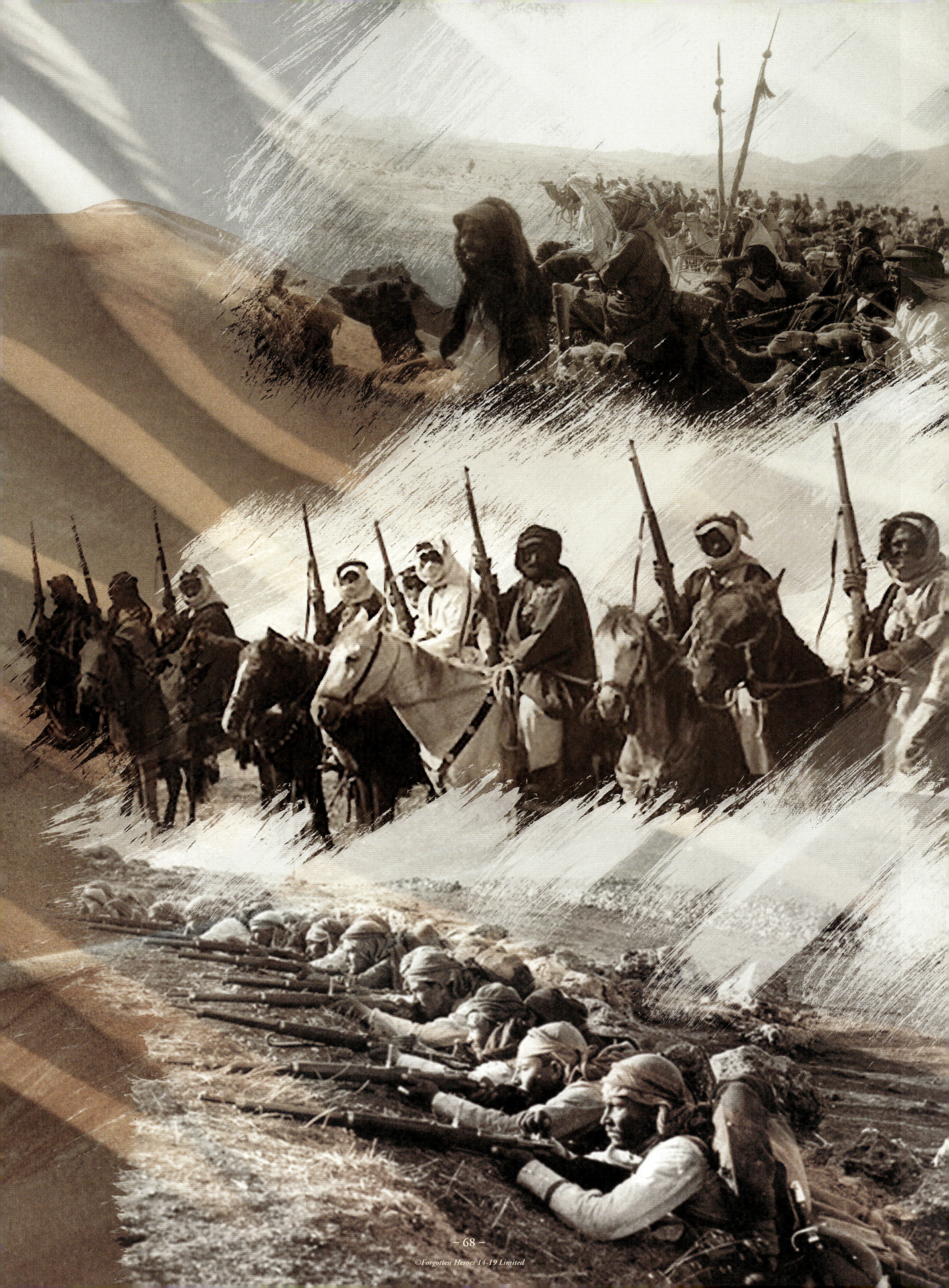

©Forgotten Heroes 14-19 Limited

> *If you tell the truth, you don't have to remember anything.*
> Mark Twain

Le 9 mai 1915, **la Division Marocaine** s'illustre lors de la bataille de l'Artois. Unité la plus décorée de la Grande Guerre, elle reste méconnue. Lors de la Grande Guerre, cette unité comptait en effet dans ses rangs des zouaves, des tirailleurs tunisiens et algériens ainsi que des légionnaires, mais aucun marocain. Elle s'appelle ainsi car elle a été formée au Maroc en août 1914.

Le 9 mai 1915, à 10 h, après un bombardement d'artillerie, l'assaut est donné. Le 7e régiment de tirailleurs algériens et le 1er régiment étranger de la Division marocaine s'élancent de leurs tranchées vers leur objectif. Très vite, ces soldats traversent le Bois de la Folie et poursuivent leur avancée sur plus de quatre kilomètres. *"À 11h15, la côte 140 est occupée"*, raconte Pierre Montagnon. *"C'est pratiquement la première fois que le front est percé. Les légionnaires et les tirailleurs voient devant eux la plaine de Lens, mais ils sont épuisés."*

Mais ce beau succès se transforme en quelques heures en un incroyable fiasco. Alors que les liaisons télégraphiques sont impossibles, des messagers, appelés coureurs, sont envoyés pour prévenir l'état-major et demander des renforts. *"Malheureusement, ils ne sont pas crus car cela paraissait trop beau pour être vrai. Les grands patrons se sont dit qu'ils se trompaient et qu'ils ne savaient pas lire une carte,"* résume Pierre Montagnon. Le soldat Blaise Cendrars se souvient aussi avec amertume de cette victoire avortée et décrit le *"manque de jugeote et manque de foi de la part des états-majors."*

Isolés au cœur des lignes ennemies, les hommes de la Division marocaine n'ont pas d'autre choix que de se replier. Ils poursuivent les combats durant les deux jours suivants, mais sans réussir à reprendre de nouveau la côte 140. Il faudra attendre avril 1917 pour que les Canadiens s'emparent de la crête de Vimy. Les journées du 9, 10 et 11 mai sont à marquer d'une pierre rouge. Le 7e régiment de tirailleurs algériens a perdu à lui seul 50 officiers et plus de 1 900 sous-officiers et soldats.

9 May 1915. **The Moroccan Division** was renowned for its bravery during the Battle of Artois. This, the most decorated unit of the Great War, remains unknown. During the Great War, this unit counted in its ranks Zouaves, Tunisian and Algerian tirailleurs as well as legionnaires, but no Moroccan. It is called so because it was formed in Morocco in August 1914.

On 9 May 1915, at 10a.m., after an artillery bombardment, the assault was launched. The 7th Algerian Tirailleurs Regiment and the 1st Foreign Regiment of the Moroccan Division left their trenches for their goal. Very quickly, these soldiers crossed the *"Bois de la Folie"* and continued their advance of more than four kilometres. *"At 11.15, Hill 140* coast was occupied,"* said Pierre Mech. *"This was almost the first time the forehead was pierced. The legionnaries and the tirailleurs see before them the plain of Lens, but they are exhausted."*

But in a few hours this great success turned into an incredible fiasco. While telegraph links were impossible, so messengers, called runners, were sent to warn the General Staff and to request reinforcements. *"Unfortunately, they are not believed because it seemed too good to be true. The superiors said they were mistaken and could not read a map,"* says Pierre Mech. Private Blaise Cendrars also recalled with bitterness this aborted victory and described the *"lack of gumption and lack of faith on the part of the staff."*

Isolated in the heart of enemy lines, the men of the Moroccan Division had no choice but to retreat. They continued the fight for the next two days, but did not succeed in occupying Hill 140* again. They would have to wait until April 1917 for Canadians to take over Vimy Ridge. The days of 9 to 11 May are to be marked in red. The 7th Algerian Tirailleurs Regiment alone lost 50 officers and more than 1,900 NCOs and soldiers.

*Hill 140 = Vimy Ridge

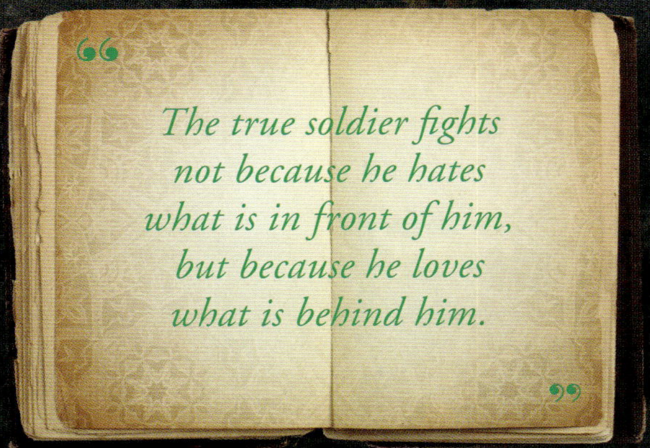

> *The true soldier fights not because he hates what is in front of him, but because he loves what is behind him.*

Of the 22 Muslim soldiers known to have fought for **Canada** in the First World War, only the 23-year-old Hasan Amat, died and his name was engraved on the Canadian National Vimy Memorial. He fell in the Battle for Hill 70 in France fighting for the 1st Battalion of the Canadian Expeditionary Force. His body was never recovered. The battle in August 1917 lasted 10 days and ended with 9,000 Canadians killed in action.

Canadian War Museum historians suspect there were many more Muslim soldiers who enlisted with the Canadian Expeditionary Force but who may have registered themselves as Church of England or similar (without denouncing their religious beliefs) for a variety of reasons, including avoiding persecution.

All Muslim soldiers served with honour and dignity.

Private Hasam Amat
Died: August 20, 1917

Regimental Number:	1075269	Survived War:	No
Force:	Army	Regiment:	Canadian Infantry
Battalion:	1st Battalion	Company:	
Place of Birth:	Singapore, Malay	Country:	Singapore
Next of Kin:	Janam Amat, sister, Arab Street, Singapore, Malay	Address at Enlistment:	Singapore, Malay
Date of Birth:	January 1, 1894	Trade or Calling:	Seaman
Marital Status:	Single	Prior Military Experience:	No
Place of Enlistment:	Halifax, Nova Scotia	Date of Enlistment:	January 14, 1916
Age at enlistment:	22	Height:	5 Feet 2 Inches
Chest:	35 Inches	Expansion:	3 Inches
Religion:	Other - See Notes	Enlisted or Conscripted:	Enlisted
Saw service in:	Europe		
Cause of Death:	Killed in Action	Battle Died/Wounded:	
Date of Death:	August 20, 1917	Age at Death:	23
Buried at:	Vimy Memorial, Pas de Calais, France	Plot:	
Commemorated:			
Prisoner of war:	No	Interned:	
Gender:	Male	Ethnic Origin:	Not Specified
LAC Reference: RG 150, Accession 1992-93/166, Box 1Box 130-34			
Canadian Virtual War Memorial Commonwealth War Graves Commission			

Rank	Regiment	Unit
Private	Canadian Infantry	1st Battalion
Private	Canadian Infantry	Royal Canadian Regiment

Religion specified as Muslim. Also served as Regimental No. 478860.

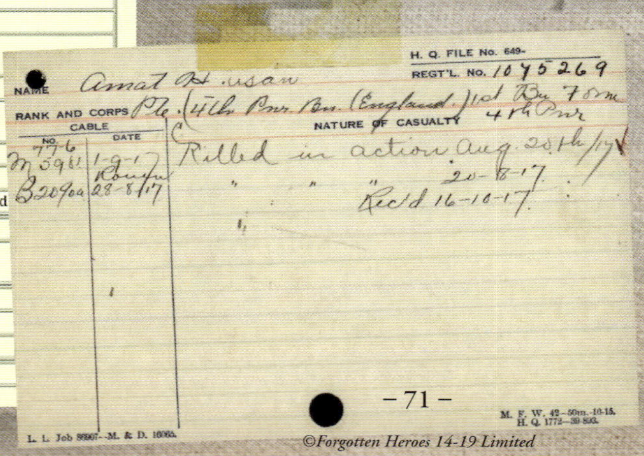

VIMY RIDGE
APRIL 9-12, 1917

- Allied Artillery Batteries
- Narrow Gauge Tram Line
- Town
- Battalion Advances
- Canadian Subways
- German Trenches

Source: Canadian Historical Section G.S.

Start	4th August 1914
End	11th November 1918
Canada's Population	8 million
Canadians who served (men and women)	630,000
Who went overseas	425,000
Canadians killed	60,661
Canadians wounded	172,000
Major Battles (Canadian involvement)	2nd Ypres (1915) St Eloi (1916) Mont Sorrel (1916) Somme (1916) Vimy Ridge (1917) Hill 70 (1917) Passchendaele (1917) Amiens (1918)

MARRIED SINGLE yes WIDOWER
TRADE OR CALLING Seaman RELIGION Mohammedan
DESCRIPTION.
APPARENT AGE 22 YEARS 6 MONTHS
HEIGHT 5 FEET 3 INCHES
CHEST MEASUREMENT 33 INCHES EXPANSION 3½ INCHES
COMPLEXION Black EYES Brown HAIR Black
DISTINGUISHING MARKS Nil

MEDICAL EXAMINATION. PLACE St. Andrews. N.B DATE June 28th 1916
Present Address Singapore Malay Pen,

—72—

*Photograph of Sam Hussein Unis and his army buddies training at Fort Sheridan, Georgia. A veteran of World War I, Sam was drafted only four months after he arrived in America in 1917. Immigrants who served in the war were given US citizenship Courtesy of Don Unis.

The **United States of America** entered the war in 1917, almost three years after European powers had been bludgeoning themselves to near destruction. 4,5 million Americans served, among them more than 5,000 Muslims. The name Muhammad was so common that it was spelled 41 ways in military records.

According to Amir Muhammad, the author of *Muslim Veterans of American Wars* and the co-founder of the Islamic Heritage Museum, in Washington, DC, these soldiers could trace their origins to Afghanistan, Albania, Algeria, the Arabian Peninsula, Egypt, Lebanon, Morocco, Persia, Syria, Tunisia, Turkey, and Yemen.

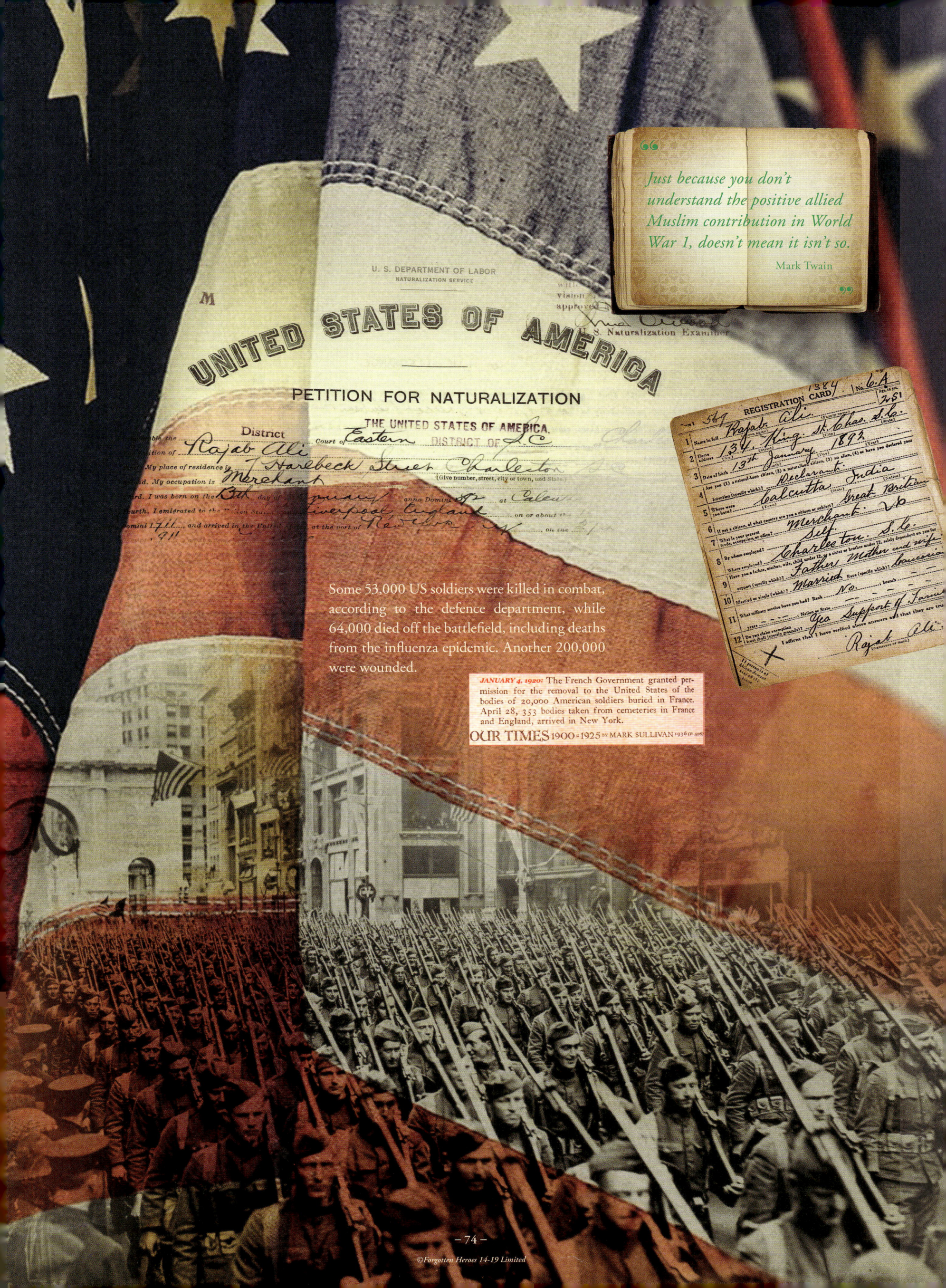

> *Just because you don't understand the positive allied Muslim contribution in World War 1, doesn't mean it isn't so.*
>
> Mark Twain

Some 53,000 US soldiers were killed in combat, according to the defence department, while 64,000 died off the battlefield, including deaths from the influenza epidemic. Another 200,000 were wounded.

JANUARY 4, 1920: The French Government granted permission for the removal to the United States of the bodies of 20,000 American soldiers buried in France. April 28, 353 bodies taken from cemeteries in France and England, arrived in New York.

OUR TIMES 1900–1925 BY MARK SULLIVAN 1936 (P. 508)

> *Nothing in this world is harder than speaking the truth, nothing easier than flattery.*
> — Fyodor Dostoyevsky

A widely accepted scholarly estimate is that between 1 million and 1,5 million Muslims (Tatars, Bashkirs, Meshcheriaks and Teptiars) were called up to serve in the **Russian** Army, accounting for nearly 10 per cent of the army's total strength.

Historians have yet to shed much light on this subject.

For Muslims, special food was prepared that excluded pork products, while the traditional glass of vodka on naval or military ceremonial days was substituted with tea and sugar. When the Unit buglers sounded the tattoo, Muslim soldiers rolled out their prayer mats for the namaz (evening prayer).

At the end of July 2016, when Muslims were celebrating the festival of Eid al-Fitr (Uraza Bairam) following the end of the sacred fast, the Petrograd Akhun Baiazitov sent a message to Tsar Nicholas and received the following answer: *"I thank you and all the Muslims who have gathered for the prayer service to mark the festival of Uraza Bairam, for your prayers and your expression of loyal feelings. I highly value the prowess of those many Muslims who are fighting in the ranks of our brave army."* (signed Nicholas)

FIRST MASURIAN CAMPAIGN
Movement After Tannenberg and Operations to 13 September 1914

GALICIAN BATTLES
Opening Movements; Situation on 1 September; Austrian Retreat to 26 September 1914

NORTHEASTERN EUROPE, 1914
Operations on Eastern Front to 26 September 1914

About 140,000 **Chinese** worked for American, British and French troops in Europe, Africa and Mesopotamia, and up to half a million Chinese workers labored on the eastern front for Russia, before the empire crumbled in the 1917 Communist revolution.* A substantial amount of these workers were Muslim.

Though not soldiers, they were subjected to military and battlefield discipline. Working and living conditions were not only harsh but fraught with danger. Often, they found themselves operating at the frontline even in the trenches facing enemy fire. They were poorly equipped and inadequately protected since few knew or understood the deadly warfare they were in.

A major Muslim population, *the Hui (Chinese Muslims)*, has lived in China for centuries, and China's rulers actively worked with them to cultivate relations with the broader Islamic world in order to pursue a variety of national goals. From the reign of the late Qing (1870-1912) through the Republic (1911-1949) and up to the Cultural Revolution (1966-1976), Islam was an important, if underappreciated, component of the self-perception and foreign relations of three different Chinese states.

(Estimated Hui population in 2011: 10 million)

> *When you are laboring for others, let it be with the same zeal as if it were for yourself.*
> — Confucius

*Historian Li Zhixue of Jinan University and Hong Kong University historian Xu Guoqi

DIRECTORATE OF GRAVES REGISTRATION AND ENQUIRIES.

TECHNICAL INSTRUCTIONS.
Revised to 1st Feb., 1918.

Chinese.

The ideal site to secure repose and drive away evil spirits is on sloping ground with a stream below, or gully down which water always or occasionally passes.

The grave should not be parallel to the north, south, east or west. This is specially important to Chinese Mohammedans. It should be about 4 ft. deep, with the head towards the hill and the feet towards the water. A mound of earth about 2 ft. high is piled over the grave.

The graves will be registered under the orders of the Director of Graves Registration and Enquiries, but the Chinese should also be allowed to mark them by erecting a wooden tablet at the foot of the grave, stating the name, age, province and village in China of the deceased. The O.C. Group Headquarters will render to the D.A.D.G.R. & E. of the Army or L. of C. area concerned, a burial return showing the registered number and date of death of every Chinaman dying in his Group. The Graves Registration Unit concerned will then erect a stake bearing the registered number of the Coolie and the date of death.

Whenever possible, the friends of the deceased should be allowed access to the corpse, and should be allowed to handle it, as they like to dress it and show marks of respect.

Comité d'Assistance aux Victimes Belges de la Guerre

Le Caire, le _____ 1916

The Belgian King Albert I and Queen Elisabeth visiting Cairo (Egypt) in 1930 to express their gratitude for the Egyptian contribution in the war.

Letters were traced confirming that the Egyptian people made a substantial donation to the Belgian Red Cross in 1916 in which Queen Elisabeth was serving as a nurse at the battle front.

1914 – 1918

ONE HUNDRED AND NINETY TWO MEN
OF THE EGYPTIAN LABOUR CORPS
ARE BURIED NEAR THIS SPOT

On 2 November 1914, General Sir John Maxwell, the commander of British forces in **Egypt**, declared martial law and pledged to spare the people of Egypt any role in the war. *"[Great Britain] takes upon herself the sole burden of the present war without calling upon the Egyptian people for aid therein."*

British war planners came to regret Maxwell's sweeping promise, for the war proved longer and bloodier than anyone had imagined, and started recruiting Egyptian laborers to meet the manpower needs on both the Western and Middle Eastern fronts.

A Memorandum* on Egypt's Contribution to the War, provides the total number of Egyptian natives recruited for service with the British Army from 17 March 1917 to 30 June 1918:

Egyptian Labour Corps *(in France, Iraq, Salonika, Mudros, Mesopotamia and Aqaba)*	237,407
Imperial Camel Corps	530
Camel Transport Corps	2,686
Horse Transport, A.S.C.***	14,057
Veterinary Service	7,207
Remount Service	5,312
TOTAL	327,199

These workers served with distinction and the Egyptian press gave glowing reports on the contributions of the Egyptian Labor Corps to the war effort. They served in supply and assisted with digging and reinforcing trenches. Yet the Egyptian workers faced great hardship in Europe. The winters were far harsher than any they had ever experienced, they were exposed to daily dangers, and sanitary conditions were poor, giving rise to disease. Many died or went missing, compounding the suffering of their families on the home front.

According to Dr Ashraf Sabri** approximately 1,000,000 Egyptian soldiers fought in the Middle East with the British forces against the Ottoman Empire, but further research needs to be undertaken.

> *Stripped to the waist and sweated chest. From trenches deep towards the sky. Non-fighting troops and yet we die.*

---

* *FO 371/3199/68122 Memoranda on Egypt's Contribution to the War, Enclosure 5.*
** *Professor of Military History at the Nasser Military Academy, Cairo Egypt*
*** *Army Service Corps.*

> *The death of an elderly man is like a burning library.*
> — African proverb

The mobilisation for war occurred during Ramadan 1914. This presented the French with some challenges in **West Africa** as the majority of their African soldiers were Muslim.

The French deployed between 500,000 and a million troupes indigenes in Europe. At least half were Muslim. Their service in Europe on such a large scale led to a rethink of the way Islam was seen by the predominantly Christian countries which governed the African territories. Because West Africa was more diverse in its religious beliefs and practices, it was easier to incorporate into French war aims than North African Islam. In addition to serving in Europe, French Africans were also to serve in the Balkans, Dardanelles and the German African territories of Cameroon and Togoland.

British West Africa (Nigeria, Ghana, Sierra Leone, the Gambia) provided two military formations: West African Regiment in Sierra Leone and West African Frontier Force (WAFF). The WAFF was mostly Hausa, a group said to be a *"warlike Mahommedan race not purely negroid."* At least 5,000 of the 8,000 WAFF were Nigerian. The Gold Coast (Ghana) Regiment saw a total of 9,890 men serve in World War 1. Of these 64% were from the Northern Territories of whom 14% were Muslim, the majority following local animalist traditions. These formations saw service in West Africa, fighting alongside the French in Cameroon and Togoland before a select group from Nigeria and Gold Coast (Ghana) were sent to East Africa from late 1916.

All three colonial powers recognised the importance of religious differences in West Africa. The Germans under Cameroon Governor Karl Ebermaier circulated letters claiming the war was a religious one and that the Germans were fighting for the cause of Islam. Support was also sought from Muslim leaders such as Garoua in Northern Cameroon. The French, who were most concerned about uprisings, eventually created mixed contingents on the Western Front with a white battalion serving alongside a West African one. North African regiments were mixed with European settlers from North Africa. Unrest had been developing because of the stringent French centralisation policies. By mixing battalions the French hoped they could stop defections to the German and Ottoman Empires. The British appear to have had the least issue with religious affiliation, there being no obvious distinction between the regiments.

The British awarded a total of 124 African Distinguished Conduct Medals to those who served in West Africa, at least 38 (30%) were Nigerian Muslims who fought in Cameroon.

Dr Anne Samson

The campaign which was fought in **East Africa** between 8 August 1914 and 25 November 1918 saw at least 177 micro-nations involved in the conflict, an estimated 1,300,000 men, of whom around one million were porters.

Exact numbers for the British forces are not available, although the King's African Rifles was said to contain a large percentage of Muslims. RV Dolbey records that the Gold Coast and Nigerian contingents who fought in East Africa from October and December 1916 respectively, were: *"Very, very smart and soldier-like these Hausa and Fulani troops; Mohammedan, largely, in religion..."*. Zanzibar, an Ismaili sect, raised a transport corps and the Zanzibar Volunteer Defence Force. There were no Muslims in the Belgian Force Publique and very few, if any, amongst the Indian Police force which served in Portuguese East Africa.

Religion did not determine loyalty; Muslims, alongside Christians, fought for both sides despite the jihad called by the chief Sunni authority and leader of the Ottoman Empire. The Aga Khan reminded his Ismaili followers that *"the Mohammedan religion commands its adherents to be loyal to their sovereign and by this is meant the British Raj."** At least three Arab Corps are known to have served in East Africa. One British under Arthur Wavell, *"a professing Mohammedan… who had made the pilgrimage to Mecca."*

Both sides used Islam for propaganda purposes to little avail in East Africa. For the Germans, actions such as flying the crescent moon above forts and bomas were attempts to keep their askari loyal and the populace peaceful, whilst for the British recognising Islamic events and festivals would not be remiss. Neither side succeeded in fomenting major unrest in the opposing force.

Whilst the white forces were predominantly Christian, many of the black, Arab and Indian forces were Muslim. The two religions fought alongside each other and in the same regiments, Christian officers and Muslim rank and file, dependent on one another for survival.

A total of 42 African Distinguished Conduct Medals were awarded during the campaign. Of these six were awarded to Muslims.

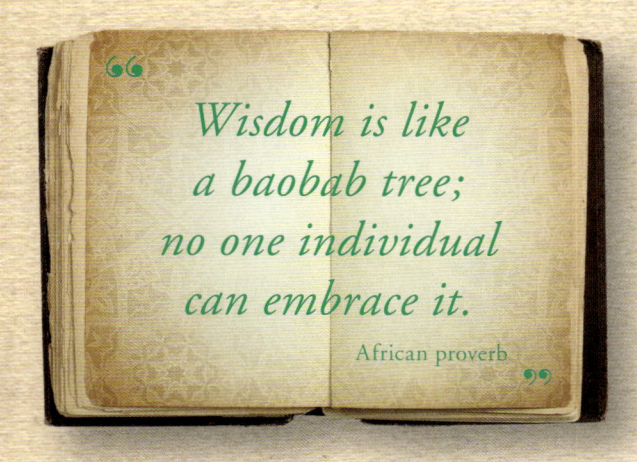

> *Wisdom is like a baobab tree; no one individual can embrace it.*
> — African proverb

Dr Anne Samson

*Paice, 2007: 212

King's African Rifles.
BRITISH EAST AFRICA.
Photo: Bink

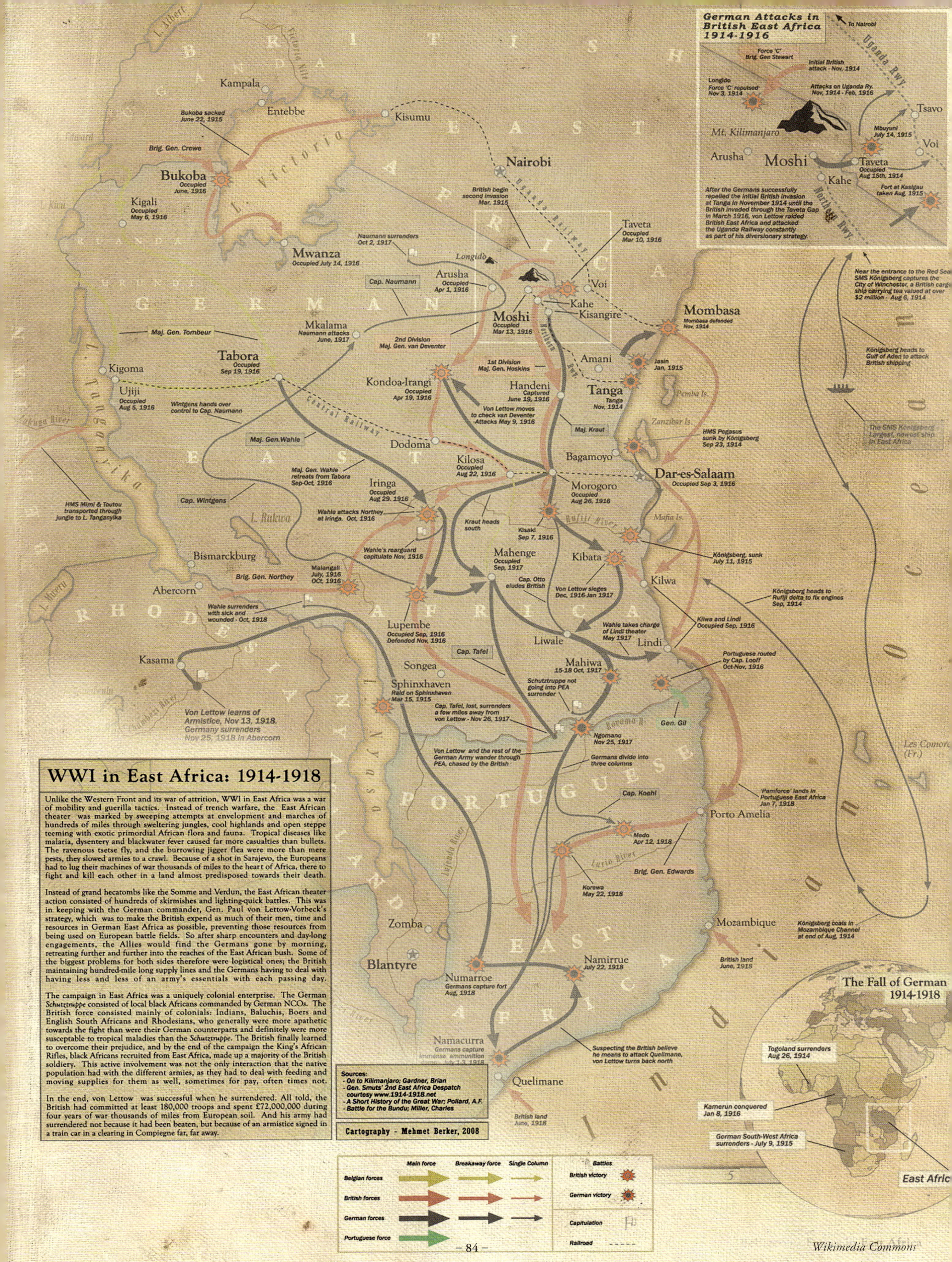

WWI in East Africa: 1914-1918

Unlike the Western Front and its war of attrition, WWI in East Africa was a war of mobility and guerilla tactics. Instead of trench warfare, the East African theater was marked by sweeping attempts at envelopment and marches of hundreds of miles through sweltering jungles, cool highlands and open steppe teeming with exotic primordial African flora and fauna. Tropical diseases like malaria, dysentery and blackwater fever caused far more casualties than bullets. The ravenous tsetse fly, and the burrowing jigger flea were more than mere pests, they slowed armies to a crawl. Because of a shot in Sarajevo, the Europeans had to lug their machines of war thousands of miles to the heart of Africa, there to fight and kill each other in a land almost predisposed towards their death.

Instead of grand hecatombs like the Somme and Verdun, the East African theater action consisted of hundreds of skirmishes and lighting-quick battles. This was in keeping with the German commander, Gen. Paul von Lettow-Vorbeck's strategy, which was to make the British expend as much of their men, time and resources in German East Africa as possible, preventing those resources from being used on European battle fields. So after sharp encounters and day-long engagements, the Allies would find the Germans gone by morning, retreating further and further into the reaches of the East African bush. Some of the biggest problems for both sides therefore were logistical ones; the British maintaining hundred-mile long supply lines and the Germans having to deal with having less and less of an army's essentials with each passing day.

The campaign in East Africa was a uniquely colonial enterprise. The German Schutztruppe consisted of local black Africans commanded by German NCOs. The British force consisted mainly of colonials, Indians, Baluchis, Boers and English South Africans and Rhodesians, who generally were more apathetic towards the fight than were their German counterparts and definitely were more susceptible to tropical maladies than the Schutztruppe. The British finally learned to overcome their prejudice, and by the end of the campaign the King's African Rifles, black Africans recruited from East Africa, made up a majority of the British soldiery. This active involvement was not the only problem the native population had with the different armies, as they had to deal with feeding and moving supplies for them as well, sometimes for pay, often times not.

In the end, von Lettow was successful when he surrendered. All told, the British had committed at least 180,000 troops and spent £72,000,000 during four years of war thousands of miles from European soil. And his army had surrendered not because it had been beaten, but because of an armistice signed in a train car in a clearing in Compiègne far, far away.

Sources:
- On to Kilimanjaro; Gardner, Brian
- Gen. Smuts' 2nd East Africa Despatch courtesy www.1914-1918.net
- A Short History of the Great War; Pollard, A.F.
- Battle for the Bundu; Miller, Charles

Cartography - Mehmet Berker, 2008

> *I learned that courage was not the absence of fear, but the triumph over it. The brave man is not he who does not feel afraid, but he who conquers that fear.*

In August 1914, the Union of **South Africa** entered into World War 1 along with Britain and its dependencies. The Union Government offered to defend its borders allowing the Imperial Garrison to return to Europe.

Of more concern for the ruling white population was the internal security of the territory, where whites were outnumbered by blacks. For this reason, people of color were not to be armed. This, however, did not stop the various South African communities, of all colors, offering their support to the British Empire.

The Muslim population in South Africa was small. The 1911 Census records 62 whites who declared themselves Muslim and 45,904 Cape Malay of whom 99.5% were Muslim. The Cape Malays constituted 0.8 per cent of the total population.

In September 1914, when Turkey sided with Germany, the Malay community formed the Malay Ambulance Corps for service in German South West Africa. According to Bill Nasson, they asked to carry arms in order to *"repel 'barbaric Sultans and their merciless tribes',* and to protect the wounded from the *'repulsive'* and *'uncivilised Turks who respect not the home of the sick'."*

The later declaration of jihad in November had no impact on South African allegiance other than to cause *"some introspection over wartime loyalty in more Turkish influenced mosques in Cape Town."*

In 1915, the South African Government agreed to the Colored Cape Corps serving in East Africa. Their use was supported by the Muslim-led African People's Organisation.

Where the Muslims stood was further expressed in a telegram, sent on 26 October 1917, by the Chairman of the British Muslim League in Durban, Jeewa, to the Governor General in Pretoria: *The Muslim League representing the Muslims of Natal and having many members of Basutoland Rhodesia and Elsewhere beg to offer heartfelt condolences to their Excellencies and family for the sad bereavement of their only son. His fine sacrifice in the cause of the worlds liberation should serve as a splendid example to the youths of the empire. His revered memory shall always remain immortal.*

Dr Anne Samson
British Library Buxton Papers

Forgotten Heroes

Forgotten are those who died
They came in from every side
We come together to learn
Each one attending in turn

We are told the stories of soldiers
Who stood by shoulder to shoulder
They did not fear their destiny
They wrote a letter of testimony

The final place of rest
After all they tried their best
To fight for that what is right
And leave gravestones for our sight

We remember them and feel sad
They did good but we feel bad
The many untold stories
Of many who claimed no glory

Rukhsana Hussain, Leicester

> *Commemorating World War 1 is not about military victory. It is about education on peace, mutual respect and humanity.*

"Our journey to The World War 1 battlefields and graveyards of Northern France was an emotional and rewarding experience full of soul searching, remembrance and self-discovery that is permanently etched in our hearts. Muslims were there too, along with the brotherhood of man in faith, culture and nationality."*

*Yusuf Chambers
Photographer: Rooful Ali

King George of the British Empire greeting Spahi soldiers on the battlefield in France

British armed forces paying tribute to the Muslim soldiers cemetery in Woking, United Kingdom

King Albert I of Belgium saluting North African soldiers in Veurne, Belgium

> *Remember that these men are not just statistics: they were people just like we are, with the same hopes, dreams & very imminent fears.*

French remembrance monument dedicated to the Muslim contribution. Douaumont, France

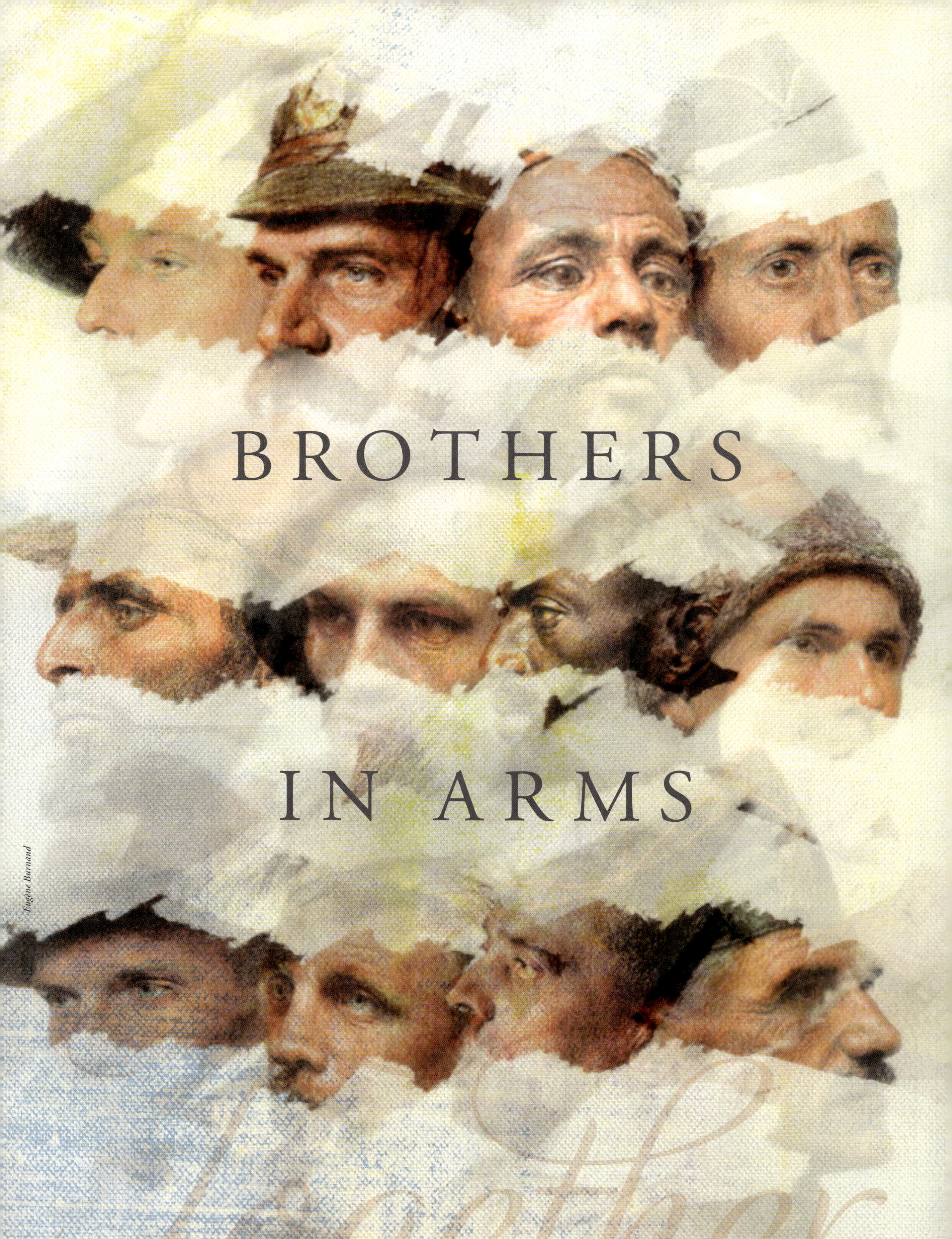

BROTHERS

IN ARMS

Eugène Burnand

TOGETHER

WE STAND

FRENCH

Where does this soldier come from? Where did he get the acuity of gaze, the severe and distinct profile under his legionnaire's helmet? Is he Breton, Picard or Provencal? It matters not. Above all he is French. On his faded coat collar the number 37 certifies that he belongs to one of the famous regiments of the Iron Division, one of those that France was counting on from the first hours. Even though the storm was rumbling on the horizon, he went. He bivouacked on the slopes of the Great Couronné, on the edge of Lorraine's woods, in the valley where the river Seille meanders. And then he was taken to all the battles. Everywhere, as he says in his own rough language, where there was a "show", he was there in the front line. From the low hills of Morhange to the mud in Artois, from the desolate plateaus of Verdun, menacing under the snow, during the great push to the caverns of the Chemin des Dames, the XXth Corps gave freely its strength and its life. If he belonged to one of the typical divisions of the French Army, this soldier of the 37th who opens the series of heroes of the Great War is also chosen as the epitome of the soldier type who is now honored after so much neglect and suffering.*

AUSTRALIAN

This handsome young man, beautiful as an ancient athlete, one of the heroes sculpted on the metopes of the Parthenon, a classical beauty, is born of a race without history, a beautiful flower thrust out, far from the passions of old Europe under the big sky of Australia. With slender body, supple limbs and frank gaze, he works all his muscles, in a country that fashions itself. One day, anxious for the world, he had to do something more. The Australian battalions, jaunty under their turned-up hats, disembarked in France. And straight away went into combat. In Flanders, on the Somme, they were everywhere, in all the attacks. In them, there was confidence on the days of attack, going forward without hesitation, and on days of retreat, making the sacrifice. What was expected, and when acts of heroism became the norm, they continued to surprise everyone. They gave magnificently.*

BRITISH

Those who have not heard the firing of British artillery do not know the sound of thunder; from morning to evening, and throughout the night, all the artillery pieces bark, rumble, howl, from the field batteries to the famous 6-inch guns whose great voice dominated the din. It was said that artillerymen fired for pleasure, for the raw visual satisfaction of seeing, beyond the enemy wire, raising heavy clouds the colors of earth and sulphur. They themselves, calm under the replying German shells, got on with their hard job, khaki breeches and gaiters, tunic off, just in shirts, sporty and tidy at the worst moments. The clean shaven face, under the flat helmet, this artilleryman has something childlike and mystical in his blue eyes which sometimes gives to these modern troopers the unexpected appearance of archangels. And, the battle done, he will leave on the paved roads of Flanders, following the wonderful machinery, sanded, gleaming, polished, singing a quiet Tipperary, as a man pure in body and spirit, who knew about fighting courageously and about dying, if it were necessary, as a gentleman.*

Ce beau jeune homme, beau comme un athlète antique, comme un des héros sculptés aux métopes du Parthénon, beau d'une beauté classique, est né d'une race sans histoire. C'est une belle fleur poussée d'un seul jet, loin des passions de la vieille Europe, sous le grande ciel de l'Australie. Le corps délié, les membres souples et le regard sand détour, il a travaillé de tous ses muscles, dans un pays qui se forme tout seul. Puis un jour d'angoisse pour le monde, il a fallu faire plus et mieux. Les bataillons autraliens, crânes sous le chapeau relevé, ont débarqué en France. Et on les a tout de suite emmenés au combat. En Flandre, sur la Somme, on les a vus à toutes le batailles, à toutes les attaques. Ils étaient de ceux à qui on faisait confiance le jours d'offensive, pour aller de l'avant sans hésiter – aux jours de repli, pour le sacrifice. Ils ont manifiquement donné ce qu'on attendait d'eux et dans un temps où l'héroisme même devenait banal, ils ont étonné le monde.

D'où vient-il, ce soldat? Ou a-t-il puisé l'acuité de son regard, la ligne sévère et pure à la fois de son profil, sous le casque légionnaire? Est-il breton, picard ou provençal? Qu'importe. Il est avant tout francais. Au col fané de sa capote, le numéro 37 atteste qu'il fait partie d'un de ces régiments fameux de la Division de fer, une de celles sur quoi la France comptait dès la première heure. Aussi bien l'orage grondant à l'horizon, il est parti. Il a bivouaqué aux pentes du Grand Couronné, aux lisières des bois de Lorraine, dans la vallée ou la Seille noue et dénoue son souple ruban. Et puis on l'a mené à toutes les batailles. Partout, comme il dit dans son rude language, où "se donnait le bal", il était là, et au premier rang. Des collines basses de Morhange aux boues de l'Artois, des plateaux désolés de Verdun, sinistres sous la neige, lors de la grande ruée, aux creutes du Chemin des Dames, le XXme corps a donné, sans compter, de forces et de vies. S'il fait partie d'un des "corps types" de l'Armée française, le soldat du 37me, qui ouvre la série des héros de la Grande Guerre, est bien aussi le "soldat-type", celui qui est à l'honneur après avoir été si longtemps à la peine.

Ceux qui n'ont pas entendu tirer l'artillerie britannique ignorent le bruit du tonnerre; du matin au soir, et la nuit durant, toutes les pièces aboyaient, grondaient, hurlaient, depuis les batteries de campagne jusqu'aux fameux obusiers de six pouces dont la grande voix dominait le vacarme. On eût dit que les artilleurs tiraient pour leur plaisir, pour l'après joie de voir, au-delà des fils de fer ennemis, monter les lourds nuages couleur de terre et de soufre. Eux-mêmes, calmes, sous la riposte des obus allemands, vaquaient à leur dure besogne, culottés te guêtrés de kaki, mias tunique basse et en chemise, sportifs et bien tenus aux pires moments. La face strictement rasée, sous le casque plat, cet artilleur garde dans ses yeux bleus quelque chose d'enfantin et de mystique qui donne parfois à ces troupiers modernes d'inattendues figures d'archanges. Et, la bataille calmée, il s'en ira sur les routes pavées de Flandre, au pas des merveilleux attelages, poncés, luisants, astiqués, chantant un vague Tipperary, en homme net de corps et d'esprit, qui sait se battre en brave et mourir, s'il le faut, en gentleman.

- 93 -

©Forgotten Heroes 14-19 Limited

AUSTRALIAN
Robert Hamilton

FRENCH
Desvignes

BRITISH
G W Kimberley

Eugène Burnand

The English translation is based on the original notes from the artist, written between 1915 and 1919 and even if some testimonies may sound awkward for people today, the painter was in full admiration of the men he painted and meant no offence in any way.

GURKHA

He is a warrior, by race and tradition, for whom since the beginning of time there is no other reason to live. He fights in the army of the Emperor of India, with the same valor deployed by his ancestors in the wars they conducted over past centuries. Though he wears the British uniform and the turned-up hat, his chinstrap underlines a unique and oriental face, prominent cheekbones, narrowed eyes, stiff mustache, a Mongolian face, recalling nearby China. The Gurkhas have given England a magnificent contingent, never weary, always ready to undertake the toughest tasks. On the high plateaus of India, in the ancient landscapes of the world, it seems they drank at a spring giving endless strength, vitality and courage.*

VC winner Kulbir Thapa, 2/3 Gurkha Regiment, first Gurkha to win Victoria Cross, 1915. He was one of 3 - George Wheeler, 9 Gurkha Regiment (1917) and Karanbahadur Rana, 3 Gurkha Regiment (1918).

C'est un guerrier, un guerrier de race et de tradition, pour qu'il n'est pas d'autre raison de vivre depuis que le monde est monde. Et il combat dans l'armée de l'Empereur des Indes, avec la même valeur que déployaient ses ancêtres dans les guerres qu'ils ont menées pendant des siècles. S'il porte, l'uniforme britannique et le chapeau relevé, sa jugulaire souligne pourtant une face orientale et singulière, des pommettes saillantes, des yeux bridés, des moustaches raides, un masque mongol, qui rappelle la Chine toute proche. Les Gurkas ont donné à l'Angleterre un contingent magnifique, jamais las, toujours prêt et aux plus rudes tâches. Sur les hauts plateaux de l'Inde, dans les plus vieux paysages du monde, il semble qu'ils aient bu à une source sans fond d'énergie, de vitalité et de courage.

SCOTTISH

We think of them as traditionally shown: the clan tartan, the kilt, bare knees and regimental mascots, dogs, white goats and those incredible regimental bands, the bagpipe whose tunes evoke the melancholy of misty Scotland. And behind all this fine show: for months on end, the bare legs of the Scots trod the mud of Flanders, the bagpipes droned the withdrawal of Haig, Smith-Dorrien and Robertson when the British Army fell back in good order, they sang the victory songs after the Marne, in the virtually ruined villages where they rested on leaving the trenches. For the brave men, they played the old tunes of bonny Scotland, of mists, lakes the color of pearls, the country of poets and soldiers. In the clear eyes of the Scotsman, a beautiful dream appears. He fought heroically, in all sectors of Belgium, Artois, Picardy, where the war was more ghastly than elsewhere; but when he stepped down for a rest, clear conscience, the corps complete, he walked down the roads, kilt flapping on muscular knees, thinking of his homeland far away, and under his short mustache, humming a little bagpipe tune.*

Nous les imaginions toujours tels que nous les montre la tradition: le paid aux couleurs du clan, le kilt, les genoux nus et les bêtes fétiches du régiment, les chiens, les chèvres blanches et ces fanfares étonnantes, les big-pipe dont les refrains évoquaient toute la mélancolie de la brumeuse Ecosse. Et voici qu'il y avait autre chose derrière ce beau décor de pompe: les jambles nues des "scotts" ont, pendant des mois et des mois, pataugé dans la boue liquide des Flandres: les cornemuses ont rythmé de leur aigre musique le pas de soldats de Haig, de Smith Dorrien, de Robertson, quand l'armée britannique se repliait en bon ordre; elles ont chanté des chansons de victoire apres la Marne; dans les villages le briques aux trois quarts ruinés, où l'armée se reposait au retour des tranchées, elles ont, pour tous ces braves, joué les vieux airs du beau pays des bruyères, des lacs couleur de perle, du pays où naissent les poètes et les soldats. Dans les yeux clairs de cet Ecossais, passe un beau rêve. Il s'est battu en héros, dans tous ces secteurs de Belgique, d'Artois, de Picardie, où la guerre se faisait plus affreuse qu'ailleurs; mais quand il descendait au repos, la conscience sans tache, le corps net, il s'en allait sur les chemins, le kilt battant ses genoux musclés, songeant à sa lointaine patrie avec, sous sa courte moustache, un petit fredon de cornemuse.

RUSSIAN

The Slav soul, of which it seems to have been said, is found complete, exotic and striking in the pure face of this young man. The Cossacks are definitely not only bearded giants, launched at an infernal gallop on their tiny horses, slashing and whipping with equal strength, enemy squadrons and rioting crowds. One also finds among them spiritual souls, mystical and gentle, eyes lit by visions of peace, their minds full of the gospel of Yasnaya Polyana. When the big day dawned, these men were not the last to respond to the Tzar's call, nor the least keen to fight, or the least heroic facing death. Under Astakhan hats, their head held high despite the storm. And now, when their country faces dark times, what do they think of those beautiful fraternal doctrines whose sinister caricature terrifies the world?*

L'ame slave, dont il semble qu'on ait tout dit, se retrouve entière, exotique et prenante sur le pur visage de ce jeune homme. Les Cosaques, décidément, ne sont pas seulement des géants barbus, lancés au galop infernal de leurs petits chevaux, sabrant et fouettant avec une égale énergie les escadrons ennemis et les foules d'émeute. On trouve aussi parmi eux des âmes inclinées, mystiques et douces, des yeux éclairés de visions paisibles, des esprits tout pleins de l'évangile d'Isnaïa Polyana. Quand vint le grand jour, ces hommes ne furent pas les derniers répondre à l'appel du tzar, ni les moins ardents au combat, ni les moins héroïques devant le mort. Sous leur bonnet d'astrakan, leur tête s'est maintenue droite sous l'orage. Et, maintenant à l'heure où leur pays sombre dans la nuit, que pensent-ils de ces belles doctrines de fraternité dont la caricature sinistre épouvante le monde?

GURKHA

SCOTTISH
NCO

RUSSIAN
Makieh Chichkine

Eugène Burnand

Brothers

The English translation is based on the original notes from the artist, written between 1915 and 1919 and even if some testimonies may sound awkward for people today, the painter was in full admiration of the men he painted and meant no offence in any way.

BRITISH

The old English infantry, the most tenacious, most steadfast in the world. It had the most glorious past possible: it was the infantry of Malplaquet, of the Peninsular wars, of Waterloo, the infantry of Marlborough and Wellington. We have learnt often — to our cost — that it held against all the assaults, against the onslaughts. It was disciplined and traditional, proudly holding on to the memories of glorious times, marching slowly behind the flags whose colors had always flown above to the music guiding the march. All that the world knew, and that it would play an important part in the storm that hit. In the rush of the first weeks, all the great British regiments, with heroic names, were ready to stand fast without faltering. But who would have thought that after these old faithful troops, would come more and more free men to defend liberty? Who would have thought that the New Army would be able to adapt so quickly to modern warfare, flexible, responsive to the demands made of them. The soldiers of Ypres, Messine, Vimy and Cambrai have shown the enemy that faith in the justice of a cause, in the honor of the nation, was able to sweep away all prejudices, all habits and in a few months create a formidable force.*

La vieille infanterie anglaise, la plus tenace, la plus inébranlable du monde. Elle avait le passé le plus glorieux qui se pût: c'était l'infanterie de Malplaquet, des guerres de la Péninsule, de Waterloo, l'infanterie de Malborough, de Wellington. Nous avions appris souvent — à nos dépens — qu'elle tenait contre tous les assauts, contre toutes le charges. Elle était diciplinée et traditionnelle, conservant pieusement les souvenirs de sa gloire, marchant d'un pas lent derrière les drapeaux dont les couleurs avaient toujous flotté sur elle, au rythme d'une musique qui, toujours avait scandé son pas. Tout cela, le monde le savait et que sou l'orage qui allait s'abattre, elle ferait belle figure. Et de fait, sous la ruée des premières semaines, tous les beaux régiments britanniques, aux noms héroïques, se firent tuer sans défaillance. Mias qui aurait cru qu'après ces vieilles troupes fidèles, il en viendrait tant et tant d'autres, formées de tous ces hommes libres venus pour défendre la liberté? Qui aurait cru que cette armée nouvele saurait si vite s'adapter à la guerre moderne, s'assouplir, se plier à toutes les exigences? Les soldats d'Ypres, de Messine, de Vimy, de Cambrai, ont montré à l'ennemi que la foi dans la justice d'une cause dans l'honneur de la nation, pouvait balayer tous les préjugés, toutes les routines et créer en quelques mois une force à quoi rien ne résiste.

PORTUGESE

José D'Azevedo Lobo da Veiga (1891-1973) was a musician, pianist and composer, who stayed in France after the war for a few years and eventually returned to a successful career as a concert pianist and composer, including a film score and recordings. Burnand describes how he entertained a family on their piano, playing frenetic arpeggios, and marches that were befitting a cinema. Born in Lagos, Algarve, Portugal. Portugal entered the war in March 1916 and sent an expeditionary force of 55,000 to France in 1917. Portugal also sent two expeditionary forces to Africa in 1914 and another two in 1916.

Small, dark, lively in all his movements, in gestures, dressed in a soft grey uniform, he has left his sun-drenched country, where palm trees rise in the clear air, where the gold colored wine matures next to the sea. With his brothers he set up in the trenches of Picardy, with nothing to break the view but trunks of apple trees, savagely decapitated, nothing but the undulating plain, punctuated with low ruins. He has persevered through the rain, snow, shell-fire and if the great tide has swept him away, he voluntarily brought to a holy cause, hard work, sacrifice and if necessary his life.*

Petit, noir, vif, tout en mouvement, en gestes, vêtu d'un souples uniforme gris, il a quitté son pays de lumière, où les palmiers montent dans l'air limpide, où le vin coleur d'or mûrit devant la mer. Avec ses frères on l'a installé dans les tranchées de Picardie, sans que rien put distraire sa vue que les troncs des pommiers, sauvagement décapités, rien que la plaine ondulée, jalonnée de ruines basses. Il a tenu là sous la plaine, sous la neige, sous les obus et si la grande marée l'a balayé, il n'en a pas moins volontairement apporté à une cause sait des efforts, des sacrifices et sa vie s'il avait fallu la donner.

TOIKENESE

An unusual face, a glimpse of the exotic is captured in the taut features, the sallow skin and almond-shaped eyes. The Orient is at our side, lush forests, full of animals, fever-ridden swamps, smell of decay, the fiery sun and warm rain, all debilitating, what must men who come from this be thinking? Certainly we have seen them, recognise them as they have come in to our towns, wearing our military uniforms, but who can penetrate their inner thoughts which suggest a secret behind their narrow eyes? What can our psychology of culture make of the mysteries of ancient Asia now before us?*

L'etrange figure, l'étrange vision d'exotisme aperçue dans ce mufle tendu, dans cette peau huileuse, dans ces yeux bridés. C'est tout l'Orient lointain qui se dresse à nos côtés, la forêt profonde, pleine de bêtes, le marécage d'où monte la fièvre l'odeur de corruption, et le soleil de feu et la pluie chaude, plus déprimante encore. Que doivent penser les hommes qui vivent dans ce décor, cous ce ciel? Certes nous le avons vus, nous les connaissons, ils sont venus dans nos villes et la guerre les a revêtus de nos uniformes, mais qui pénètrera le secret de leur visgae fermé qu'éclaire seul l'éclat furtif de leurs minces yeux? Que peuvent les subtilités de notre psychologie et notre culture devant le mystère de la vielle Asie soudain apparu tout entière devant nous?

PORTUGESE
José D' Azevedo Lobo da Veiga

BRITISH
Edward Roland Parker

TOIKENESE
Lai Van Chau

*The English translation is based on the original notes from the artist, written between 1915 and 1919 and even if some testimonies may sound awkward for people today, the painter was in full admiration of the men he painted and meant no offence in any way.

CANADIAN

Canada gave the British Army the most faithful, valiant, and most tireless contingent. From the great prairies stretching as far as the eye can see to the verdant horizon, their velvet fields brightened with specks of sheep, from dense woods animated by the furtive life of furry animals, from lakesides, immense plains, bounding rivers, from the solitude of the Rocky Mountains, came the men, loyal to their home country. The old French blood, flowing in the blood of many, the old warrior blood reawakens, mixed with fertile British vigour, and the soldier appears, taut muscles, ready and willing. Within these blended races, diversities enhance each other. Sometimes they are augmented with Native American ancestry. And when a man feels the triple flow of blood, French, British, Native American, he presents to the world the most magnificent example of tenacious courage, timely zeal and flexibility: the most complete type of soldier.*

Le Canada a donné à l'Armée britannique le contingent le plus fidèle, le plus vaillant, le plus infatigable. Des grandes prairies prolongeant à perte de vue leurs horizons de verdure, leur velours égayé des taches claires des troupeaux, des bois épias animés de la vie furtive des animaux à fourrure, du bord des lacs des plaines immenses, des rivières bondissantes, des solitudes perdues des Montagnes Rocheuses, sont venus les hommes, pour apporter à la Métropole l'hommage de leur loyauté. Le vieux sang français qui coule dans les veines de plus d'un, le vieux sang guerrier s'est réveillé, mêlé à la féconde sève britannique et le soldat a paru les muscles tendus, la volonté prête. Dans ces races composites, diverses, les vertus se complètent et s'élargissent. Elles s'augmentent parfois d'éléments étrangers, d'ascendances indiennes, Et quand l'homme sent battre son coeur au triplr flux du sang français, britannique, indien, il peut présenter au monde le plus magnifique exemple de courage tenace, d'ardeur à la fois et de souplesse: le type le plus complet du soldat.

BELGIAN

The Antwerp fortress was one of the most powerful in Europe, the bastion of the Belgian Army. But what could the marvels of fortification do against the blasts of the 420s, against the incessant attacks by the enemy? Antwerp taken, after a heroic resistance, Germany believed Belgium was defeated. But Germany failed to recognise the Yser. It was not master of the king, the army, the people; it was not master of the spirit of the country. Noble, chivalrous race for whom honor is supreme. It is real, vibrant, in the face of this sound Belgian officer, with his powerful coarsely-hewn features. In the eyes, a direct look, the expression of a soldier and a knight. This defender of Antwerp epitomises the defence of right over wrong, ceaselessly on the verge of being overwhelmed by the tempest, always returning from the brink, stronger and indefatigable.*

La forteresse d'Anvers était une des plus puissantes d'Europe, c'était le réduit de l'armée belge. Mais que pouvaient les merveilles de la fortification contre les rafales des 420, contre la marée incessante de l'ennemi? Anvers pris, après une belle résistance, l'Allemand crut la Belgique à terre. Mais il comptait sans l'Yser où on l'arrêta. Il tenait la place, il n'était pas maitre di Roi, de l'armée, du peuple; il n'était pas maitre de l'âme du pays. Noble race chevaleresque pour qui l'honneur passe avant toutes chose. Elle apparait réelle, vibrante, sur le visage de cet officier belge ferme, aux trait puissants taillés à larges traits. Dans les yeux un regard droit, un regard de soldat et de chevalier. Ce défenseur d'Anvers incarna la défense du droit contre la force, sans cesse à la veille d'être submergé sous la houle de la tempête, sans cesse renaissant; toujours plus fort et invoilable désormais.

ITALIAN

It is impossible to be more Italian and moreover like a policeman. Additionally great style, under the large hat on askew, that for so many years has been the emblem of all the constabularies of Europe. A combined air of firmness and calm, a clear rustic expression. He is a northern Italian, of that old mountain race which united and brought fame to the Kingdom. Steadfast in his role, dedicated and with a tenacious hatred of imperialism, he served thankless in the towns of the plains: in Padua, Verona, Venice. Then was sent to France, with the Italian contingents. In the camps, on the roads, on station platforms, one saw beside the caps of our police the carabinieri hat. It has become a familiar wartime silhouette, a sheepdog for soldiers on leave, ordered and disciplined, he is good natured and sympathetic. He has loyally worked for victory, and his praises were well-deserved, placing him among the brave.*

Il n'est pas possible d'être plus italien, et plus gendarme, par surcroit. Belle allure d'allures, sous le grand chapeau en bataille qui, pendant tant d'années, a été l'emblème de toutes les maréchaussées d'Europe. L'air ferme et pacifique à la fois, un regrd clair de paysan. C'est un Italien du nord, de cette vieille race montagnarde qui a fait l'unité et la gloire du royaume: solide à son poste et vouant aux Impériaux une haine tenance. Il a fait son ingrat service d'arrière dans les villes de la plaine: à Padoue, à Vérone, à Venise. Puis on l'a envoyé en France, quand les contingents italiens y sont venus. Dans les cantonnements, sur les routes, aux quais des gares, on a vu à côté du casque de nos gendarmes, le grand chapeau du carabinier. Il est devenu une des silhouettes familières de la guerre, chien de berger du troupeau des permissionnaires, correct et dicipliné, il est bon enfant et sympathique. Il a été un loyal artisan de la victoire, et l'hommage lui était bien dû, qui le place parmi le braves.

CANADIAN
C E Parker

BELGIAN
De Witte

ITALIAN
Gualco Giuseppe

Eugène Burnand

*The English translation is based on the original notes from the artist, written between 1915 and 1919 and even if some testimonies may sound awkward for people today, the painter was in full admiration of the men he painted and meant no offence in any way.

FRENCH

One can imagine him in every kind of headgear with which the centuries have successively endowed the troops: he is the eternal soldier-type; one can see him under the bearskin, under the morion, the toque, the helm; one sees him wearing the winged helmet of the ancient Gauls, whose strong features he shares, accentuated by his fabulous mustache. Thus he is the embodiment of the French race in all its most solid and vigorous characteristics, a race born from the land and endlessly drawing new strength from it, this land which has had to be periodically defended against Barbarians. The unity of the country is so fine and its harmony so perfect, that the same native valor lights the eyes of all its sons, whether they come from the plains of Flanders, the broom and gorse of Brittany or the hillsides of Burgundy. France, that miraculously varied country, has found itself at one again: the same blood has beaten in all its hearts, the same enthusiastic shouts have filled all its mouths, the same firm confidence has inspired every will.*

On l'imagine sous toutes les coiffures dont les siècles ont successivement doté les soldats: il est le soldat éternel; on le voit sous le bonnet d'ourson, sous le morion, la toque, le heaume, on le voit sous le casque ailé des vieux Gaulois, dont il a les traits puissants, soulignés des moustaches légendaires. Ainsi il incarne la race française dans ce qu'elle a de plus solide, de plus vigoureux, race née de la terre, et y repuisant sans cesse des forces nouvelles, de cette terre qu'il faut périodiquement défendre contre les Barbares. L'unité est si belle, l'harmonie si parfaite de notre pays, que les mêmes vertus natives éclairent les yeux de tous ses fils, qu'ils viennent des plaines de Flandre, des garrigues du Languedoc, des genêts bretons ou des côteaux de Bourgogne. La France, diverse à miracle, s'est retrouvée une; le même sang a battu dans tous les coeurs, la même clameur d'enthousiasme a empli toutes les bouches, la même foi a fixé toutes le volontés.

AMERICAN

The immense rimmed hat, tied with a multi-colored cord, astonished us initially and worried us a little. It recalled for us cinema cowboys and a galloping Buffalo Bill. But only a short while after their arrival, the Americans had already shown they were accomplished organizers and heroic soldiers. They passed by on the Lorraine roads and their lines of lorries extended interminably. In doorways, children crammed together to watch the foreign soldiers pass, clean shaven and nimble, and as a result there was between children and troops the most cheerful friendship that endured until the last day. The "Sammies" when billeted, were the most good natured in the world, without any of the inconsiderate noise that was too often the expectation. Pockets full of sweets and cigarettes, they were the benefactors of children and the tobacco deprived. They hung around with the girls, flirting respectfully and bilingually and animated the land with their boyish cheer and charm. With the war finished and the task accomplished, specific interests turned to high level talking, let us remember that they have been, much more than allies, more even than comrades, friends.*

Ce chapeau immense à bords plats, noué d'une cordelette bigarrée, nous étonnait au début et nous inquiétait un peu. Il rappelait à nos yeux les cow-boys de cinéma et les galopades de Buffalo-Bill. Mais, bien peu de temps après leur arrivée, les Américains se montraient déjà organisateurs accomplis et soldats héroïques. Ils passaient sur les routes de Lorraine et leurs camions s'allongeaient en files interminables. Devant les portes, les enfants s'entassaient pour voir passer les soldats étrangers glabres et prestes et de suite ce fut entre marmots et troupiers la plus joyeuse camaraderie qui dura jusqu'au dernier jour. Les "Sammies" étaient au cantonnement les meilleurs enfants du monde, sans rien du sans-gêne bruyant qui les a trop souvent fait mal juger. Les poches pleines de bonbons et de cigarettes, ils étaient la providence des moutards et des fumeurs en mal de tabac. Ils prolongeaient avec les jeunes filles des flirts repectueux et bilingues et animaient le pays de leur gaité puérile et charmante. Si la guerre finie et la tâche accomplie, les intérêts particuliers se sont mis à parler haut, sachons nous rappeler qu'ils ont été pour nous, bien plus que des alliés, même que des camarades: des amis.

SIKH NCO
Sunder Sing Haldice

The Indian Army was the pride of England, perhaps it has been its salvation. At the start, when the old British regiments were upholding their reputation by being ground down while waiting for other divisions pushing hastily towards them, the Hindus had a heavy task. These men of sun lived and died in the mud. They secured for themselves, under the grey skies of Flanders, eternal glory. The Sikhs were particularly wonderful. For centuries, in the high valleys that climb towards the Himalayas, they were free and warriors, proud of their customs, of their heritage, of their religion. England found amongst them its best soldiers, and in fact, against Germany, they were incomparable. It is sufficient to see them to recognize in them the sons of a warrior race. Look at this man; weather beaten face, the energy in his eyes which tells us he is a soldier; the short rolled beard lifted ritually to the top of the head, remembering ancestral traditions, which give honor and strength to nations.*

L'armée des Indes était l'orgueil de l'Angleterre, peut-être a-t-elle été son salut. Au début, quand les vieux régiments britanniques eurent soutenu leur réputation d'héroisme en se faisant hacher, en attendant que d'autres divisions pussent accourir, les Hindous eurent une lourde tâche. Ces hommes de soleil vécurent et moururent dans la boue. Ils s'assurèrent, sous le ciel gris des Flandres, une gloire éternelle. Les Sikhs notamment firent merveille. Depuis des siècles, dans les hautes vallées qui montent vers l'Hymalaya, ils étaient libres et guerriers, fiers de leurs coutumes, de leur passé, de leur religion. L'Angleterre trouvait parmi eux ses meilleurs soldats, et de fait, contre l'Allemand, is furent incomparables. Il suffit de les voir pour reconnaitre en eux les fils d'une race de guerre. Voyez cet homme: le visage basané, les yeux d'énergie disent le soldat; la courte barbe roulée, relevée rituellement vers le sommet de la tête rappelle les vieilles traditions des ancêtres, cells qui font l'honneur at la force des peuples.

FRENCH
Valezar

AMERICAN
Miller

Eugène Burnand

SIKH NCO
Sunder Sing Haldice

Brothers

*The English translation is based on the original notes from the artist, written between 1915 and 1919 and even if some testimonies may sound awkward for people today, the painter was in full admiration of the men he painted and meant no offence in any way.

> *If not us, then who?*
> *If not now, then when?*

Acknowledgements

When I created the Forgotten Heroes 14-19 Foundation, more than six years ago, I never expected being asked to publish a book with the aim of reaching out to grassroots communities worldwide, providing a glimpse of our findings. It wasn't to be an academic or historical database, but a visual coffee table book focused on the human aspects of all the Allied Muslim soldiers.

We had long and intensive discussions within our team about whether or not we were able, because the only thing we had achieved over the six years was locating and identifying approximately 850,000 unknown, presumed lost archives and personal documents dedicated to the Allied Muslim contribution. Only a fraction (less than one percent) had been translated and analysed due to a lack of funding and manpower.

But young people can be very persuasive, and we finally agreed, not least because we also received unexpected financial support from a few individual Muslims. Humble men with no titles, no wealth but a sincere belief in humanity and the same message we were trying to communicate. May God bless them and their families.

The thousands of men and woman who have been recording the events of World War 1 to the best of their abilities and the anonymous heroes who have been, and still are, working in the archives of public and private institutes, often in harsh circumstances, the world owes you so much. Thank you.

It goes without saying that the archives would have been useless if a legion of devoted researchers and historians had not sacrificed fortune and social lives to ensure that this aspect of world history would never be forgotten. I've had the privilege to meet some in person, but most of them have reached out to me with marvellous books. Treasures that we mention in our Further Reading section, and which are a must for all who care about history. We have done our utmost to mention all the books my team and I have been reading, and I apologize for those we have forgotten. We will certainly mention them in our next volume.

Whilst you might not agree with all the books listed, they're part of the journey to the truth.

We also would like to thank the hundreds of civil servants, diplomats, secretary generals, military officers, ministers, princes and even a king who took the time to hear about our project while we were traveling around the world. Doors to archives were opened that would still have been locked without their help.

There would of course be no book without the amazing advice and expertise of designer Kate Wells, our editor Dr Anne Samson and the dozen individuals, collectors, journalists and institutes who have donated unique archives or given us permission to use their material.

And last but not least, we are so lucky to have this inner circle of brave dynamic heroes who have been with us on the battlements to create this book as an independent, non-political, non-governmental, non-religious organisation. Thank you Hayyan Bhabha, Yusuf Chambers, Rémi Letoffe, Imran Nanlawala and Nabia Khan. May God watch over you and your families for centuries to come.

Vera Mathys - Luc Ferier

Further Reading

ABBOT, Peter. 2002. *Armies in East Africa 1914-1918 (Men-at-Arms)*. Osprey.

ANTONIUS, George Habib. 1938. *The Arab Awakening: The Story of the National Movement.* London, Amish Hamilton.

ANDERSON, Ross. 2004. *The Forgotten Front: The East African Campaign 1914-1918*. Tempus.

ARMSTRONG, Karen. 2008. *The Charter of Compassion.* Anchor.

BARR, James. 2014. *A Line in the Sand. Britain, France and the Struggle that Shaped the Middle East.* Simon & Schuster.

BARR, James. 2008. *Setting the Dessert on Fire: TE Lawrence and Britain's Secret War in Arabia, 1916-1918.* WW Norton.

BARTHAS, Louis. 1978. *Les Carnets de Guerre de Louis Barthas, Tonnelier, 1914-1918.* Librairie François Maspero.

BASU, Shrabani. 2015. *For King and Another Country: Indian Soldiers on the Western Front 1914-18.* Bloomsbury.

BEKRAOUI, Mohammed. 2009. *Les Marocains dans la grande Guerre 1914-1919.* Publications de la Commission Marocaine d'Histoire Militaire.

BROWN, Malcom. 1996. *The Somme.* Pan Books in association with The Imperial War Museums, London.

BOUGAREL, Xavier, BRANCHE, Raphaëlle and DRIEU Cloé. 2017. *Combatants of Muslim Origin in European Armies in the Twentieth Century. Far from Jihad.* Bloomsbury.

CAMPBELL, I Elena. 2015. *The Muslim Question and the Russian Imperial Governance.* Bloomington: Indiana University.

CHASSEAUD, Peter. 2013. *Mapping the First World War. The Great War Through Maps from 1914-1918.* Collins, in association with Imperial War Museums, London.

CHANDLER, Edmund. 1919. *The Sepoys.* John Murray.

CLARK, Christopher. 2012. *The Sleepwalkers: How Europe went to War in 1914.* Penguin.

CLEMENT, Daniel. 2015. *La Brigade Marocaine Septembre 1914. Une Meurtière Odyssée.* Musée 14-18 De Villeroy.

CRONIN, David. 2017. *Balfour's Shadow: A Century of British Support for Zionism and Israel.* Pluto.

DANIEL, Ute, GATRELL, Peter, JANZ, Oliver, JONES, Heather, KEENE, Jennifer D, KRAMER, A and NASSON, Bill. *1914-1918 Online. International Encyclopedia of the First World War.* https://encyclopedia.1914-1918-online.net/article/Introduction.

DE QUESADA, Alejandro. 2013. *Imperial German Colonial and Overseas Troops 1885-1918 (Men-at-Arms).* Osprey.

FISK, Robert. 2006. *The Great War for Civilisation: The Conquest of the Middle East.* Harper Perennial.

FOGARTY, Richard S. 2008. *Race and War in France: Colonial Subjects in the French Army, 1914-1918.* John Hopkins University.

FRASER, TG. 2015. *The First Word War and Its Aftermath.* The Gingko Library.

FRASER, TG, MANGO, Andrew and McNAMARA, Robert. 2015. *The Makers of the Modern Middle East.* The Gingko Library.

GATRELL, Peter. 2005. *A Whole Empire Walking. Refugees in Russia during World War I.* Indiana University.

GRESSIEUX, Douglas. 2007. *Les Troupes Indiennes en France.* Alan Sutton.

GUOQI, Xu. 2011. *Strangers on the Western Front. Chinese Workers in the Great War.* Harvard University.

GUOQI, Xu. 2017. *Asia and the Great War: A Shared History (The Greater War).* Oxford University.

HASTING, Max. 2014. *Catastrophe. Europe goes to War 1914.* William Collins.

HAMILTON, Ian. 1920. *Gallipoli Diary.* E Arnold.

HEIKE, Liebe, BROMER, Katrin, LANGE, Katherina, HAMZAH, Dyala and AHUJA, Ravi. 2010. *The World in World Wars. Experiences, Perceptions and Perspectives from Africa and Asia.* Studies in Global Social History, vol. 5 Brill.

HERTMANS, Stefan. 2016. *War and Turpentine.* Pantheon.

HUREWITZ, Jacob Coleman. 1979. *The Middle East and North Africa in World Politics: A Documentary Record, Second Edition, Revised and Enlarged; Volume 2, British-French Supremacy, 1914–1945.* Yale University.

JACOB, Harold Fenton. 1923. *Kings of Arabia.* Mills and Boon.

JAMES, Gregory. 2013. *The Chinese Labor Corps. (1916-1920).* Bayview Educational.

JEWEL, Norman Parsons. 2016. *On Call in Africa in War and Peace 1910-1932.* Gillyflower.

JUNG, Peter. 2003. *The Austro-Hungarian Forces in World War I: 1914-1916 (Men-at-Arms).* Osprey.

KANT, Vedica. 2014. *'If I die here, who will remember me?' India and the First World War.* Roli.

KEEGAN, John. 2000. *The First World War.* Vintage.

KHALIDI, Omar. 2001-2. *Ethnic group recruitment in the Indian Army: The contrasting Cases of Sikh, Muslims, Gurkhas and others.* No.4. Pacific Affairs 74.

KNIGHT, Paul. 2012. *The British Army in Mesopotamia, 1914-1918.* McFarland.

LIEVEN, Dominic. 2016. *The End of Tsarist Russia: The March to World War I and Revolution.* Penguin.

LEPICK, Olivier. 1998. *La grande Guerre chimique (1914-1918).* Presses Universitaires de France.

LEWIS, Bernard. 1982. *The Muslim Discovery.* WW Norton.

LUDKE, Tillman. 2005. *Jihad made in Germany. Ottoman and German propaganda and intelligence operations in the First World War. Lit.* Verlag Münster, Germany.

MA, Li. 2014. *Les travailleurs Chinois en France.* CNRS Editions Alpha.

McMEEKIN, Sean. 2013. *The Russian Origins of The First World War.* Belknap.

MARTIN, Jean. 2014. *Un Siècle d'oubli.* Les Canadiens et la Première Guerre mondiale (1914-2014). Outremont, Athéna éditions.

McDOUGALL, James. 2006. *History and the Culture of Nationalism in Algeria.* Cambridge University.

McMUNN, G and FALLS, C. 1928. *Military Operations: Egypt and Palestine from the Outbreak of War with Germany to June 1917.* London, HMSO.

MEYER, James. 2014. *Turks across Empires: Marketing Muslim Identity in the Russian-Ottoman Borderlands.* Oxford University.

MOBERLY, Frederick James. 1924. *The Campaign in Mesopotamia, 1914-1918. Volume 2.* London, HMSO.

MUHAMMED, Amir. 2007. *Muslim veterans of American Wars.* Freeman.

NICOLLE, David. 1994. *The Ottoman Army 1914-1918 (Men-at-Arms).* Osprey.

NILÜFER KEFELI, Agnès. 2014. *Becoming Muslim in Imperial Russia: Conversion, Apostasy, and Literacy.* Cornell University.

NJUNG, George. 2016. "From Frying Pan to Fire: Dissenting Voices and the Anglo-French Bifurcation of WWI Cameroon, 1916-1919". Paper presented at the Anthropology, African History Workshop, University of Michigan, Fall 2016.

OMISSI, David. 1999. *Indian Voices of the Great War, Soldier's Letters, 1914-1918.* Palgrave Macmillan.

OWEN, David. 2014. *The Hidden Perspective. The Military Conversations 1906-1914.* Haus Publishing.

OWEN, Wilfred. 1965. *The Collected Poems of Wilfred Owen.* New Directions.

PATI, Budheswar. 1996. *India and the First World War.* Mounto.

PAYTON, Philip. 2015. *Australia in the Great War.* Robert Hale.

PETRONE, Karen. 2011. *The Great War in Russian Memory.* Indiana University.

PROVENCE, Michael. 2017. *The Last Ottoman Generation and the making of the Modern Middle East.* Cambridge University.

REMARQUE, Erich Maria. 1987. *All Quiet on the Western Front.* Ballentine.

ROGAN, Eugene. 1998. *Frontiers of the State in the Late Ottoman Empire: Transjordan, 1850-1921.* Cambridge University.

ROGAN, Eugene. 2009. *The Arabs.* Allen Lane.

ROGAN, Eugene. 2015. *The Fall of the Ottomans: The Great War in the Middle East, 1914-1920.* Allen Lane.

ROY, Franziska, HEIKE, Liebau and AHUJA, Ravi. 2011. *When the War Began We Heard of Several King's: South Asian Prisoners in World War I.* Germany. Social Science Press.

RUEDY, John. 2005. *Modern Algeria: The Origins and Development of a Nation. Second Edition.* Bloomington Indiana University.

SAMSON, Anne. 2012. *Word War I in Africa: The Forgotten Conflict Among the European Powers.* IB Tauris.

SAMSON, Anne. 2005. *Britain, South Africa and the East Africa Campaign, 1914-1918: The Union Comes of Age. International Library of Colonial History 4.* IB Tauris.

SAMSON, Anne. http://www.thesamsonsedhistorian.wordpress.com

SAYYID, S. 2014. *Recalling the Caliphate. Decolonisation and World Order.* Hurst.

SHARP, Alan. 2011. *Consequences of the Peace: The Versailles settlement – Aftermath and Legacy makers of the modern World series.* Haus Publishing.

SIBLON, John. 2016. *Caribbean Soldiers on the Western Front.* The African Heritage Forum.

SNOUCK HURGRONJE, Christiaan. 1915. *The Holy War. "Made in Germany".* GP Putnam's Sons.

SNOW, Peter and SNOW, Dan. 2007. *The World's Greatest Twentieth Century Battlefields.* BBC Books.

STONE, Norman. 1998. *The Eastern Front 1914-1917.* Penguin.

STRACHAN, Hew. 2003. *The First World War.* Oxford University.

STRAUSS, Edward M. 2014. *Poilu: The World War I Notebooks of Corporal Louis Barthas, Barrel maker, 1914-1918.* Yale University.

TAMARI, Salim. 2011. *Year of the Locust: A Soldier's Diary and the Erase of Palestine's Ottoman Past.* University of California.

TARAZI FAWAZ, Leila. 2014. *A Land of Aching Hearts: The Middle East in the Great War.* Harvard University.

TUCHMAN, Barbara W. 2004. *The Guns of August.* Presidio.

TUCHMAN, Barbara W. 1996. *The Proud Power: A Portrait of the World before the War, 1890-1914.* Random House.

TUNA, Mustafa. 2015. *Imperial Russia's Muslims: Islam, Empire, and European Modernity.* Cambridge University.

WAKEFIELD, Alan and MOODY, Simon. 2004. *Under the Devil's Eye. (Salonika).* The History Press.

WAKEFIELD, Alan and MOODY, Simon. 2008. *From Basra to Baghdad. (Mesopotamia).* Sutton Publishing.

WILLCOCKS, James. 1920. *With the Indians in France.* Constable and Company.

WOOD, Frances. 2016. *Betrayed Ally: China in the Great War.* Pen & Sword Military.

YAPP, Malcom. 1987. *The Making of the Near East 1792-1923.* Longman.

ZURCHER, Erik Jan. 2010. *The Young Turk Legacy and Nation Building: From the Ottoman Empire to Atatûrk's Turkey.* IB Tauris.

ZURCHER, Erik Jan. 2015. *Jihad and Islam in World War I. Studies on the Ottoman Jihad on the Centenary of Snouck Hurgronje "Holy War Made in Germany".* Leiden University.

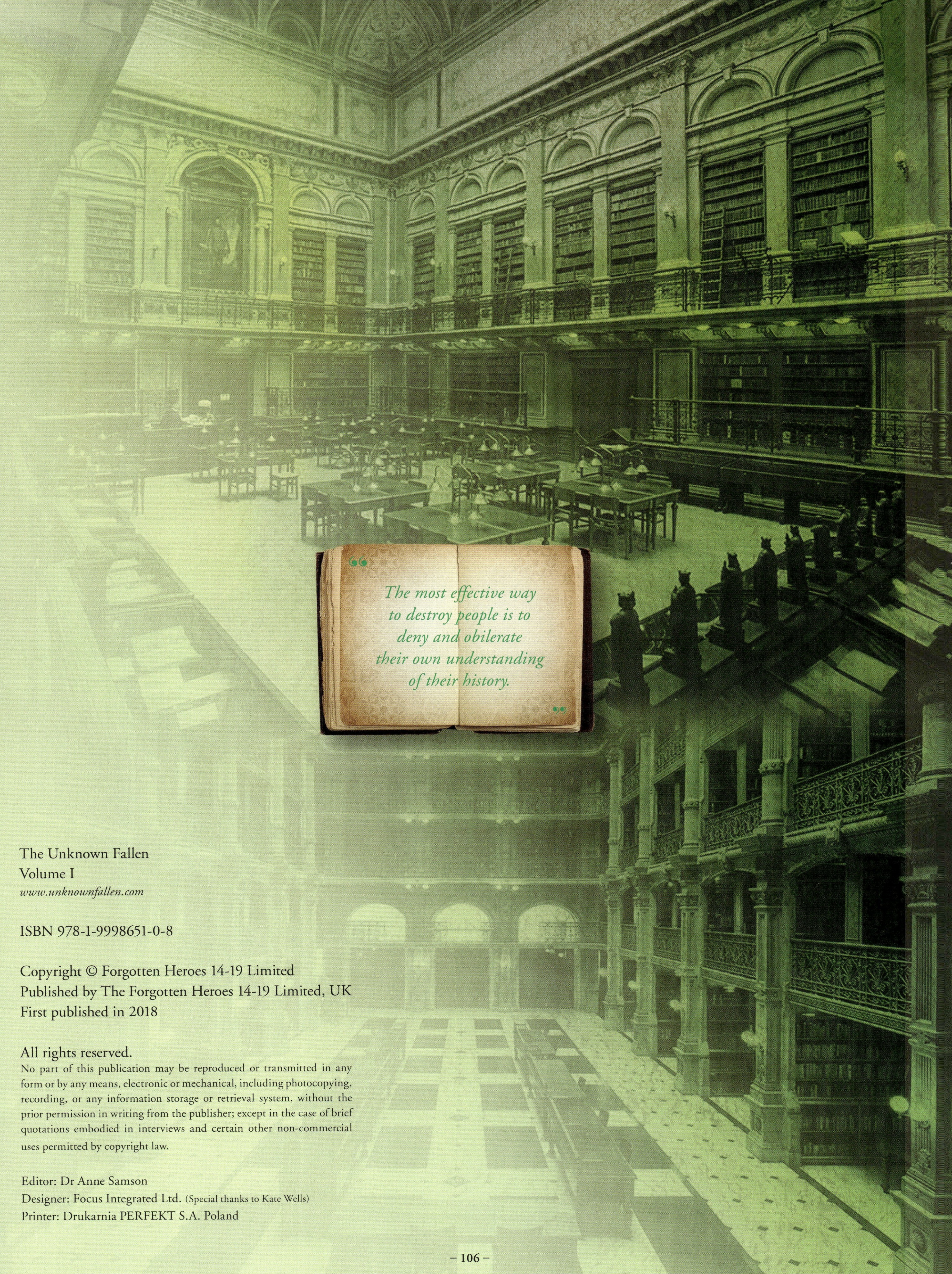

> *The most effective way to destroy people is to deny and obilerate their own understanding of their history.*

The Unknown Fallen
Volume I
www.unknownfallen.com

ISBN 978-1-9998651-0-8

Copyright © Forgotten Heroes 14-19 Limited
Published by The Forgotten Heroes 14-19 Limited, UK
First published in 2018

All rights reserved.
No part of this publication may be reproduced or transmitted in any form or by any means, electronic or mechanical, including photocopying, recording, or any information storage or retrieval system, without the prior permission in writing from the publisher; except in the case of brief quotations embodied in interviews and certain other non-commercial uses permitted by copyright law.

Editor: Dr Anne Samson
Designer: Focus Integrated Ltd. (Special thanks to Kate Wells)
Printer: Drukarnia PERFEKT S.A. Poland

©Forgotten Heroes 14-19 Limited